Mark D. Morrison-Reed

Black Pioneers
in a
White Denomination

Third Edition

Introduction by Andrew J. Young

Skinner House Books

To my wife, Donna,
and our children,
Charlotte and Elliot

Unitarian Universalist Association
25 Beacon Street, Boston, Massachusetts 02108-2800

(paperback) 9 8 7 6 5
03 02 01 00 99

Morrison-Reed, Mark D., 1949-
    Black pioneers in a white denomination /
    Mark D. Morrison-Reed ;
introduction by Andrew J. Young. — 3rd ed.
        p.   cm.
    Includes bibliographical references and
    index.
    ISBN 1-55896-250-6
    1. Brown, Egbert Ethelred. 2. McGee,
Lewis A. 3. Unitarian Universalist Association—
Clergy—Biography. 4. Afro-American
Unitarian Universalists—History. I. Title.
BX 9867.M67   1994
289.1'32'08996073—dc20   94-32438
                          CIP

Acknowledgments

The circumstances that drew this book out of me were set in motion when a colleague of my father took my parents to the First Unitarian Society of Chicago. To this act of friendship and to my parents' decision to remain I am indebted.

The process of collecting the material for this work was arduous but rewarding. The most fortuitous event was meeting with Ethelred Brown's daughter, Dorice Leslie. By the time I spoke to her, I had formed an impression of Brown that she largely confirmed. Yet, in meeting her, I gained a sense of the tragedy of Brown's life. Researching his life was a deeply emotional experience for me, and if my writing is tinged with subjectivity, it is appropriate, for not only was I disheartened by his story, but I have a heavy investment in the long-term outcome of his vision.

The writing of this work would not have been possible without the assistance and support of many people. I am thankful to my advisers, John C. Godbey, J. Ronald Engel, C. Shelby Rooks, and fellow students Jay Atkinson, Arvid Straube, and W. Frederick Wooden for reading and criticizing the manuscript, suggesting new leads and insights, and encouraging me in this project. I am indebted to numerous libraries and librarians, particularly the Meadville/Lombard Theological School Library and its librarian, Neil W. Gerdes, the Andover-Harvard Theological Library, Harvard Divinity School and its Curator of Manuscripts, Alan L. Seaburg, and the Schomburg Center for Research in Black Culture, the New York Public Library, Astor, Lenox and Tilden Foundations and Diana

Lachatanere of the Rare Books, Manuscripts and Archives Section. I am grateful to Lewis and Marcella McGee for allowing me to interview them and for reviewing and suggesting extensive changes in the third chapter. The research assistance of Michael Hennon was crucial. The thoughtful appreciation and criticism of Thomas Payne was sobering. The enthusiasm and repeated assurances of Bill Schulz that my thesis should reach a broader audience convinced me to pull it off the shelf and start reworking it. The editorial help, which came in waves, was invaluable. First were Wendy Jerome and Karen Yano. The revised edition was coaxed from me by Marie Cantlon and Gerald Charipar. And from my very first inquiry until the last word was edited, Carl Seaburg, former director of information for the Unitarian Universalist Association, aided me in every possible way.

Most importantly, I thank my wife, friend and colleague, Donna, for having patience with me as I plodded through this work and for her many contributions, including taming my awkward sentences and unique spelling.

Contents

Preface

In the beginning I didn't know who they were or where to find them. But I had heard of David Eaton. In 1976, while visiting my grandmother in Washington, DC, during the Christmas holiday, I dressed up in a sports coat and tie and drove to his church on 16th and Harvard Streets. As I slipped in the side entrance of All Souls Unitarian Church I was anxious. That faded when David saw me, smiled, threw his arms wide, and spoke my name with his mid-Atlantic drawl. Then he sat me down in his wood-panelled study and said, "Man, let me tell you how it is . . ." He was the first African American Unitarian Universalist minister I had ever met.

Another year passed and I found myself in DC again, this time interviewing Lewis and Marcella McGee. Lewis lived in retirement with his step-daughter. A quiet, gentle man, he was much more circumspect than David. Six months later Thom Payne gave me a tour of the First Church of Roxbury, Massachusetts. It seated 1,500 and had a membership of forty. That same week I was reunited with Renford Gaines. I hadn't seen him since my youth-group days at the First Unitarian Society of Chicago, where he was our advisor. Now his name was Mwalimu Imara, and he worked as a Minister-at-Large for the Benevolent Fraternity of Unitarian Churches. Ben Richardson, reluctant to meet me at all, finally agreed to have lunch in the cafeteria of Chicago's Art Institute. I came to know Ethelred Brown through a clothing box filled with his sermons that his daughter had stored under her bed. Jeff Campbell—who was teaching in a rustic, ramshackle boarding school outside Putney, Vermont—regaled me with colorful stories and old labor union songs. The letter I sent to Alvin Neely Cannon in California went unanswered. And any record of the time that Joseph Fletcher Jordan spent at St. Lawrence University was lost two generations ago when its Divinity School burned down.

In the beginning my quest to learn about African American Unitarian Universalist ministers had been strictly personal—a pilgrimage driven by deep curiosity, a yearning for wise counsel, a sense of self-preservation, and a need to pay my respects to those who had preceded me. But my quest was propelled further by the need to write a thesis.

Originally I considered exploring the controversy between the champions of integration and the advocates of Black Power within the Unitarian Universalist Association (UUA). In 1969 an event known ever after as "the Walkout" almost tore the Association apart. Nearly a decade later when I contemplated this event, the memories were still fresh, the feelings volatile, and the conflicting positions were still held with passion. I retreated and focused my research on an earlier era of UU history.

Since then, writers braver than myself have analyzed that later period. In 1977 Daniel Higgins wrote a Doctor of Ministry thesis entitled "The UUA and the Color Line." In 1983 Victor H. Carpenter's Minns Lecture was called "The Black Empowerment Controversy and the Unitarian Universalist Association, 1967-1970." In the same year the Unitarian Universalist Association's Commission on Appraisal published "Empowerment: One Denomination's Quest for Racial Justice, 1967-1982."

In the preface to the first edition of this book, former UUA President William Schulz wrote about the UUA's response to the Empowerment Controversy. "As Director of Social Responsibility for the Unitarian Universalist Association (UUA), I had yearned to help re-focus our wandering eyes on matters of racial justice. Regardless of how one viewed the controversies over race within the denomination circa 1968-1970, it appeared indubitable that with the decision in 1970 to end UUA funding of the Black Affairs Council, all effective UUA attention to racial justice ended too. Our relief translated itself into inaction. Like children with hot stoves, we shunned the burner. For us, indeed, no fire next time."

We had been burnt, but in time the UUA cautiously renewed its efforts. Under three successive presidencies, it sought to address the issue of racial justice. In 1980 the Pickett administration initiated a "UUA Institutional Racism Audit." In response to a 1985 General Assembly resolution on racism, the Black Concerns Working Group was established. With the administration of Bill Schulz, persistent and incremental change continued in staffing, extension, religious education materials, and worship resources. The Office of Racial Inclusivity came into being in 1985, and the Beyond Categorical Thinking Workshops were first offered in 1988. This weekend program is designed to help congregations in the process of seeking a minister to look beyond race, gender, sexual orientation, or physical ability.

Black Pioneers in a White Denomination argues that Unitarian Universalism is a class-bound faith. A "Survey on the Quality of Religious Life in Unitarian Universalist Congregations," issued by the UUA Commission on Appraisal in 1989, includes a demographic description of African American Unitarian Universalists that supports this argument. The 1988 survey concluded: "In socioeconomic status the African American Unitarian Universalist is very similar to the Euro-American UU, but the former's attitude toward worship is significantly different." This particular chapter from the survey, of which I was the primary author, is also included in this edition, as is an updated list of African American Universalist, Unitarian, and Unitarian Universalist ministers.

During this time of moving forward I have continued looking backward. Amid the experiences and mistakes of the past I have sought patterns on which we might build a future. Since *Black Pioneers in a White Denomination* was first written fifteen years ago, and since its revision ten years ago, I have built on its argument in two additional essays: "Where There Is No Vision, the People Perish . . ." and "How Open Is the Door? How Loud Is the Call?" which appeared in *1993 Selected Essays*, originally published by the Unitarian Universalist Ministers Association. Both are included in this new edition.

Since my quest began I've come to realize that I was really searching for more than just answers. I have also sought companionship. That desire was not mine alone. Theological students have come to me as I had gone to David and then the other African American ministers. Yet as a group, African American UU ministers have met only sporadically in the past, and there were no formalized gatherings. Often they didn't know one another.

In 1988 the UUA Department of Ministry's Affirmative Action Task Force for African American ministers sponsored a conference which took place in Washington, DC.

There the African American Unitarian Universalist Ministries (AAUUM) was founded. Since then AAUUM has become a gathering in which questions are asked and answers given. But perhaps more importantly, it is a place where answers are created. In doing so, we have moved beyond yearning for companionship to building bonds of love. This has spared us some of the isolation and pain that was the fate of the black pioneers that came before, and given us reassurance that even when life is difficult we are not alone in the struggle.

Mark Morrison-Reed
January 1994

Preface to the Second Edition

I am a black-born, Unitarian-bred minister of the liberal faith. I am an anomaly. This uniqueness has placed me in a dilemma. My allegiance is split. My long and enriching experience with Unitarian Universalism has led me to a commitment to the liberal ministry. At the same time I am proud to be an Afro-American, and I realize my fate is tied to that of the black community. The former presents itself as a calling, the latter as a fate, and both are experienced as demands. The quandary I face is twofold. First, given my chosen vocation as a minister in a white denomination, how can I serve the black community? And, second, how can I inform the Unitarian Universalist tradition through the black experience? It would be simpler for me if these communities overlapped or encompassed one another, but how is one to meet the demands of two apparently exclusive groups? As I straddle them, I feel the need for a common ground from which to address both.

This personal predicament leads me to address the general problem of the segregated nature of the liberal church. Unitarian Universalism's only significant penetration into the black community has been limited to a dozen inner-city churches. Frequently churches of the liberal faith located in urban communities are unable to attract blacks, and in other areas there are few blacks. The typical congregation has several black families at most, and often none at all. In 1968 when black involvement in the denomination was at a high point, blacks numbered 1,500 of the denomination's 180,000 members, less than 1 percent.[1] A similar pattern is found in the liberal ministry. Only twenty-three black men and women have been received into ministerial fellowship since 1889.[2] In June 1983, of 1,034 fellowshiped ministers 12 were black, and of these less than half are in or are seeking parish settlements.

This experience is not different from that of other mainline denominations. In fact, 80 to 85 percent of all black churchgoers belong to black denominations. The other 10 to 15 percent belong to all-black conventions or churches in white denominations, and probably less than 1 percent attend congregations with a racially mixed membership.[3] Since they have no all-black churches, Unitarian Universalists fall in the last, infinitesimal category. Homer Jack, secretary general of the World Conference on Religion and Peace and a founder of the Congress on Racial Equality, once aptly described Sunday morning as "the segregation hour."[4]

This reality is painful for advocates of racial equality who feel that the lack of a significant black presence in liberal religious churches indicates latent racism. In a survey released in 1973 in the book *Religion among the Unitarian Universalists,* Robert Tapp reported that racial integration was considered a major problem meriting church action in the opinions of many Unitarian Universalists.[5] Indeed, I am frequently asked how the liberal church can be made more attractive to blacks. Yet since the advent of black power, when the emphasis in the Afro-American struggle shifted from human rights to black consciousness and to political and economic power, the once sacred principle of integration is held up ambivalently, if at all. Many have not been able to reconcile integration with black autonomy, and the resulting uncertainty leads them to acquiesce in their indecision. In this post-black empower-

ment era, most liberal religionists are no longer clear enough
about their values or perceptive enough in their thinking
about race to be able to move decisively. It seems the as-
similation of the rapid changes that occurred in the sixties
and seventies is a slow process. There comes the humbling
realization that we in the church do not stand above the
social attitudes of our times, but rather flounder among
them with everyone else.

This impasse is particularly frustrating for those who
believe that the liberal religious message proclaims values
that transcend racial, cultural, and economic differences.
Many expect the substance of the liberal church to reflect
its ideals of human dignity and freedom, and its failure to
attract blacks challenges the notion that the liberal gospel
is a universal one. Unitarian Universalism continues to
appeal to a relatively narrow segment of our society, the
upper middle class. William Schulz, while serving as director for social responsibility of the Unitarian Universalist
Association, confirmed this point. He wrote, "We are, as
a movement, growing whiter and whiter, safer and more
suburban. The economics of Unitarian Universalism imply
a cocoon-like comfort while turmoil goes on about us."[6]
This raises the obvious but difficult question within the
problem of segregation: Do the black and Unitarian Universalist communities hold substantially different values,
as analysis would lead us to believe? If the answer to this
question proves to be yes, we will know, in part, why the
liberal faith has so little appeal in the black community.

The problem of segregation in all churches seems more
unfortunate when one recognizes that there is much to
gain, beyond the realization of liberal values, from racially
diverse congregations. Here there is a potential for the kind

of growth-inducing dislocation that comes from an experience that challenges the unawareness of race, an insensitivity that has made whiteness the norm. In a church with a black presence whites may experience a new self-awareness, an awareness of what it means to be white in our culture. This new self-awareness is essential, for people can only affirm others after they have truly affirmed themselves. The richness of our civilization will emerge from a recognition of and respect for difference, not out of ignorance, well intentioned or otherwise. The awakening can be initiated by hearing and appreciating the story of black Americans. Besides opening a new dimension of awareness, this story also dramatizes in our era the biblical messages of suffering and liberation. The black presence has already and would further sensitize white churches to the nature of racial oppression. When racial injustice is no longer an unfortunate yet unfelt evil but rather a personal affront, we will want to combat it aggressively. This is integration where it counts—in the pews.

If we look beyond the personal and religious context of the problem in churches of the liberal faith to the broader American context, we see that the pattern of racial segregation in which Unitarian Universalists are caught is pervasive. Robert Bellah, in *The Broken Covenant*, reveals the meaning of this at the deepest level. He asserts that myth, insofar as it "transfigures reality . . . [by providing] moral and spiritual meaning to individuals or societies," is the heart of a nation's self-perception.[7] In America, part of this self-perception is the ideal of pluralism expressed in the myth of the United States as the "melting pot."

The black community stands in stark contrast to that myth and reveals its limited scope.[8] Most Americans immigrated to this country, but the black was forcibly brought and then legally segregated from the mainstream of American life. From the black perspective, the myth of the melting pot was meaningless or, even worse, demonic for those who believed that the myth included them, for it frustrated them and destroyed their sense of self-worth. As the story of the black American emerges, we find the history of a people living essentially outside the mythic structure, a history that challenges America's fundamental self-image. This is an important step in Bellah's analysis, because if the American myth is to be renewed, a development he believes to be essential, it must begin with a true understanding of our history, and a true understanding can only arise when blacks and others have criticized and celebrated the American experience from their unique perspectives. This book, which focuses on Unitarianism in particular, is a part of this criticism of American life. Moreover, although I have written self-consciously as a Unitarian Universalist, I hope others will find that it speaks to their experience as well.

This work approaches the problem of segregation in Unitarian Universalism from a historical perspective. Two of the earliest black Unitarian ministers founded churches in the black community. Egbert Ethelred Brown founded a mission church in Jamaica in 1908 and founded another church in Harlem, New York, in 1920. Lewis A. McGee helped establish the interracial Free Religious Fellowship in Chicago's black ghetto in 1947. I will bring their experiences to bear upon the issue of segregation, because they tell the tragic story from a compelling personal perspective. Until recently people have approached the problem by asking why there are so few blacks in the liberal white church. But from that perspective one could not be sure if the de facto white composition of Unitarian Universalist congregations was the overwhelming barrier for most blacks. These two ministers brought a voice to the black community that did not have to overcome the color line, and their examples address another question: Can a black minister with the liberal religious message succeed in the black community? The answer may be no, that the message itself did not address the community and, therefore, contributed to the segregated nature of the liberal church.

The stories of these two pioneering, black liberal ministers will show that the Unitarian church remained segregated, in part, because of the predominant social reality and attitudes of the pre–civil rights era. Geographically, blacks and Unitarians were segregated into different regions and neighborhoods. Economically, Unitarians generally belonged to the middle and upper classes and blacks were kept in the lower classes. Generally, the experiences of the two groups were radically different. Neither group would have experienced the crucial sense of being at home in the other's church.

Unitarian Universalists, like members of other social institutions, need to realize the obvious, namely, that we still are class and culture bound. Brown and McGee came to Unitarianism from Methodism, which appealed to the black middle class, and the blacks they attracted in turn were the upwardly mobile who had achieved a degree of economic well-being and intellectual and emotional independence from the mores of the black community. These people had already left the black religious tradition, but were reluctant to commit themselves to another church. Seeing the liberal faith's narrow appeal in the white community, a pragmatist would have had little hope that the liberal religious message would appeal to the black community, but idealists like Brown and McGee were motivated, as I am, in part, by a personal need to reconcile these two communities. The narrowness of the Unitarian message hampered these men in their efforts to attract the black community, and one must conclude that Unitarianism remained racially segregated because it is a class-bound, culturally captive religion.

The Unitarian Universalist church and others like it will remain largely segregated until there is a twofold transformation: one in society, the other within the church. First, on a societal level, it is essential that Unitarian Universalists and other liberal religionists never forget that political and economic freedoms are the mainstay of intellectual freedom, and that inequities and injustice subsequently undermine all freedom. This realization presses us to take seriously the cliché that until all of us are free, none of us is truly free. It is a "moral imperative," then, that we commit ourselves to the establishment of a just society. The result of this endeavor will be the evolution of a society potentially more responsive to Unitarian Universalist values. Second, within the liberal church, the transformation would begin with the strengthening of our spirituality through an enriched story—a story that exposes our commitment to freedom, shakes up our class bias, sensitizes us to the needs of others, strengthens our sense of human connectedness, and, finally, inspires us to struggle with others for freedom.

Introduction

Andrew J. Young

"Can we integrate the churches?" That is the essential question that Mark Morrison-Reed examines in this volume, *Black Pioneers in a White Denomination.*

The denomination he is examining is his own, that of the Unitarian Universalist Association of North America, a predominantly white liberal religious movement in the Judeo-Christian tradition, which has one thousand congregations in the United States and Canada. His message speaks to all blacks and whites who seek equity, justice, and harmony in this nation.

Morrison-Reed speaks powerfully to the issues of both classism and racism, which affect the Unitarian Universalist church and to some degree every church or temple in America. Unitarian Universalists have long been strong advocates of civil rights. Yet, as the author notes, "Unitarian Universalism's only significant penetration into the black community has been limited to a dozen inner-city churches . . . This experience is not different from that of other mainline denominations."

Today the name of Ethelred Brown is unknown to the American public, as is the name of Lewis McGee. Yet these two men, and those who stood by their sides, accomplished something new in American history. They bridged the gulf between the black community, into which they were born, and the free religious community they embraced as adults.

Brown endured poverty and "official" neglect in establishing the Harlem Unitarian Church in New York City. McGee, in fulfillment of a long-held dream, organized the Free Religious Fellowship in Chicago's South Side. Observing the inhospitality to black people of the established liberal churches of their day, they chose in spite of risks to create new multiracial congregations in the two largest cities in North America.

Brown's saga of rejection and suffering replicated the personal history of millions of black Americans. McGee, a less-volatile man, suffered less, but knew the isolation of the black professional in an overwhelmingly white denomination. When McGee became minister of the Chico Unitarian Fellowship in California in 1961, it was the first time a black man was called as the senior minister of a predominantly white Unitarian church. How sad that it took a century for the fruit of the Civil War to be reaped in the denomination that had contributed so singularly—in the ministries of William Ellery Channing and Theodore Parker—to the cause of the abolition of slavery.

Morrison-Reed states that Unitarian Universalism "needs working-class realism," and that "the black church has long housed the spiritual element that Unitarianism needs."

The author says, "There is . . . an imbalance between the spiritual and political elements in black religion that the Unitarian emphasis on intellectual freedom can help remedy. The fatalism of the disinherited [black and worker] drive them to focus on the other-worldly rather than on justice in this world . . . Power is attributed to God, but it is not recognized that individuals are the primary conduits of His power. God is perceived as all-powerful, and people as powerless. Yet gaining power is one of the central problems in the lives of blacks, workers, and the disinherited. Having power means having the ability to assert control over one's own destiny.

"For Unitarians, generally, human participation in God's power is assumed, and for humanists, it is the primary source of power . . . Intellectual freedom is the missing element in the spirituality-dominated black church," the author concludes.

"The American story," says Morrison-Reed, "is incomplete without the black story." He is right. One may add that the American church is incomplete without the black church. Dr. Morrison-Reed's narrative demonstrates the interdependence of black Americans and white Americans in the Unitarian denomination and elsewhere in creating a truly just and inclusive society.

The civil rights movement of the sixties is a prophetic example of the power that is potential when there is integration of the churches in both mission and theology. American churches are still in need of this renewal.

Chapter One

Two American Faiths

A vast cultural and economic chasm exists between blacks and liberal religionists, preventing them from communicating easily. But have the Afro-American, the descendant of bondage, and the liberal religionist, the inheritor of freedom, anything to say to one another? Indeed, they have common concerns, freedom being the foremost among these, yet they live with this rift. This book will look at two attempts to bridge the gulf between the black and the Unitarian communities: the work of Egbert Ethelred Brown and Lewis Allen McGee.

The churches of the disinherited and the churches of the middle class are quite distinct, and H. Richard Niebuhr has attempted to identify the elements fostering their separation in *The Social Sources of Denominationalism.* He argues that "denominations ... represent the accommodation of religion to the caste system . . . The division of churches closely follows the division of men into castes of national, racial, and economic groups."[1] From this perspective, black religion and Unitarianism are simply two examples of caste divisions: Black religion is a religion of the disinherited, and Unitarianism is a religion of the middle class.

H. Richard Niebuhr agrees with Ernest Troeltsch that "the really creative, church-forming, religious movements are the work of the lower strata."[2] Niebuhr goes on to describe how these religious movements are formed and how

1

they change into middle-class churches. In the process, the form and content of the religion changes in such a way as to exclude the lower classes. He uses Methodism as an example.[3]

Niebuhr finds that the test of genuine religiousness for the disinherited is "in the spontaneity and energy of religious feeling rather than in conformity to an abstract creed." As the religion becomes that "of the fortunate and cultured and has grown philosophical, abstract, formal, and ethically harmless in the process, the lower strata of society find themselves religiously expatriated." There is a change in the world view of people who have gained a degree of economic control and a broader perspective through education. The middle class becomes increasingly concerned with the individual, since in the economic arena one's personal energy, skills, and knowledge bring success, which enhances one's sense of self-worth and power. The middle class takes on "an activist attitude toward life." By contrast, the disinherited must contend with the ways of fate, and the life of the lower classes is thus often an experience of powerlessness. What small gains are made come through solidarity and cooperation. These different life experiences lead to different religious needs. Salvation for the disinherited, according to Niebuhr, comes as an act of God's grace. Their gains are seen as an act of God's will and mercy. For the middle class, salvation tends to be seen as "the end of striving": "The content of faith is a task rather than a promise."[4] For the poor, the alleviation of their suffering is God's gift; for the middle class, good works is a sign of grace. Consequently, middle-class religion, responding to individualism, focuses on personal salvation, while the disinherited, seeking God's interven-

tion for their group, tend toward millennialism and corporate redemption.

Niebuhr's delineation of the religion of the disinherited
and that of the middle class is helpful, but he is concerned
with all of American Protestantism and his analysis,
therefore, is too broad to illuminate specifically the relationship between the black and the Unitarian communities.
We shall have to turn to the stories of two black Unitarian
ministers, Egbert Ethelred Brown and Lewis Allen McGee,
for a clearer understanding of the relationship between
these two communities. These men were black pioneers in
a white denomination who struggled to bring the message
of Unitarianism to the black community. Their efforts
have never been adequately examined, and as a conse-
quence we have not learned from their experiences.

How will the life stories of Brown and McGee help us
analyze the Unitarian predicament? James W. McClendon,
Jr., in his *Biography as Theology: How Life Stories Can
Remake Today's Theology*, proposes that an ethics of character-in-community can lead to a theological discourse,
not of calculations, but of real, personal encounters with
moral decisions. In these events, the values that moral philosophy and theology try to uncover are acted out in real-
life situations in the context of a believing community—
values that are seen, not as ideals, but as they influence
and are embodied in humanity. McClendon is concerned
with values as convictions, that is, with those values that
set the tenor of one's life: "For as men are convinced so
will they live." This is the essence of character, to act in
accordance with one's convictions. Character is developed
in community and is manifested in the "living convictions
which give shape to actual lives and actual communities."[5]

The raw data for theology are to be found in the lives of the members of the community.

The ethics of character-in-community as recounted in biography is the realm of theology.

> The best way to understand theology is to see it, not as the study about God (for there are godless theologies as well as godly ones), but as the investigation of the convictions of a convictional community, discovering its convictions, interpreting them, criticizing them in the light of all that we can know, and creatively transforming them into better ones if possible.

The source of this theology is found in "attending to lived lives," for the life story of individual members of a convictional community is the focus of investigation. McClendon then claims that "biography at its best will be theology."[6] The biographies of Brown and McGee illustrate the truth of this statement, for their lives are central to the story of liberal religion's encounter with the black community.

How does McClendon carry out his investigation, moving from biography to theology? The key to any biography is the constellation of dominant or controlling images found in that life. People understand themselves in the context of certain images and metaphors. When I identify myself as an American, specific images emerge: the Founding Fathers, the War of Independence, the flag, the pioneers, the native American, the slave. From this pool of shared images will emerge the specific images that dominate any particular life, images that reveal a person's most basic motivation and self-understanding. Such images, whether derived from Greek myth, the American democratic faith, or the Bible, are basic to human religiosity.

They are the means by which we locate ourselves in the world and comprehend the wonder that is life. Investigating these most basic questions revealed in individual lives from a particular community of faith is theology.

> Our biographical subjects have contributed to the theology of the community of shares of their faith especially by showing how certain great archetypical images of that faith do apply to their own lives and circumstances, and by extension to our own. In doing so, they make clearer the answer to a preliminary theological question, *What is religion?* Part of the answer is that it is just such use of images. By images, I mean metaphors whose content has been enriched by previous, prototypical employment so that their application causes the object to which they are applied to be seen in multiply-reflected light; they are traditional or canonical metaphors and as such they bear the content of faith itself.[7]

Although many images may be shared by various religious communities, under distinctive cultural conditions different images will be emphasized by different communities. By comparing the dominant images of Unitarianism and black religion, we can learn why these two communities have remained essentially closed to one another. Toward this goal, we will examine the images in the works of some of the major writers in these two religious traditions.

BLACK RELIGION

If there is no struggle, there is no progress. Those who profess to favor freedom, and yet depreciate agitation, are men who want crops without plowing up the ground. They want rain without thunder and lightning. They want the ocean without the awful

roar of its many waters. This struggle may be a moral
one; or it may be a physical one; or it may be both
moral and physical; but it must be a struggle. Power
concedes nothing without a demand. It never did and
never will . . . Freedom is not a gift, freedom is won
through relentless effort.

FREDERICK DOUGLASS
August 4, 1857

The dominant motif in the black American experience is
the struggle for freedom: freedom from slavery, freedom
from political and economic bondage, freedom of self-
determination, and freedom to participate fully in American life. Many scholars argue that this struggle is not only
the dominant motif of black experience but also the essence of black religion. W. E. B. DuBois wrote:

Freedom came to him [the free Negro leader as] a
real thing and not a dream. His religion became
darker and more intense, and into his ethics crept a
note of revenge, into his songs a day of reckoning
close at hand. The "Coming of the Lord" swept this
side of Death, and came to be a thing to be hoped for
in this day. Through fugitive slaves and irrepressible
discussion this desire for freedom seized the black
millions still in bondage, and became their one ideal
of life. The black bards caught new notes, and sometimes even dared to sing,—

"O Freedom, O Freedom, O Freedom over me!
Before I'll be a slave
I'll be buried in my grave,
And go home to my Lord
And be free."

For fifty years Negro religion thus transformed itself
and identified itself with the dream of Abolition,

until that which was a radical fad in the white North
and an anarchistic plot in the white South had become a religion to the black world.[8]

Cecil Cone, a black theologian, cites this passage as "typical of Dubois's tendency to reduce black religion to a political ideology and his failure to see those elements in it
that transcend political activity."[9] Dubois's bias is not surprising: He was a sociologist, not a theologian. And Cone is
right: Black religion cannot be reduced to political ideology. The image of freedom described in the work of black
writers has three dimensions: the spiritual, the political,
and the intellectual.

It is obvious that blacks should be concerned with at-
taining their freedom. It is equally clear that the church, as
the sole black institution during slavery and the only viable
institution for a long time after the Civil War, should also
be concerned with freedom, but there is much debate over
the stance the black church has taken. Many claim that
the church is too other-worldly, whereas its defenders assert it has maintained a balance between this-worldly and
other-worldly concerns.

Joseph Washington is among the deriders. In *Black Religion* he passes a harsh judgment on the black religious
institution, saying, "The churches are foremost in their
attempt to negate reality." He also perceives that Negro
folk religion, which he distinguishes from the black church,
has its own "genius," a genius that confronts the reality of
oppression. "The Negro folk religion is fundamentally and
unequivocally dedicated to freedom, expression, independence, and the rise of Negroes to equal status in the society."[10] James Cone also argues that the impetus of black
religion is toward liberation.

James Cone, the most polemic and prolific of the contemporary black theologians, argues in *God of the Oppressed* that God is and always has been on the side of the oppressed, that blackness is the ontological symbol of oppression in America, and that the reconciliation of blacks and whites can occur only after liberation. Liberation is both a prerequisite for and an act of freedom. Referring to the Old Testament Cone argues that Yahweh "is the God of history whose will is identical with the liberation of the oppressed from social and political bondage." This is the uncompromising message of the Old Testament and one that advances through the New Testament. Jesus' primary identification is with the poor, the suffering, and the outcast. The freedom he brings them is not apolitical or otherworldly: It encompasses worldly liberation and is "more than historical freedom."[11] Blacks in America became loyal to the Bible when they discovered that it spoke to their experience in slavery. No matter how the slave master abridged the Bible, he could not hide its basic message of freedom for the oppressed. The slaves' ability to see behind the corrupted Word they were taught was a critical act of intellectual freedom. Their reinterpretation of the biblical message and its incorporation into black reality through the creation of spirituals was a creative act. These are all expressions of freedom, an aesthetic freedom that helped blacks confront their harsh reality. Within bondage, blacks exercised this freedom and their minds resisted slavery.

In an earlier book, *The Spirituals and the Blues*, James Cone identifies the themes of black life as expressed in black music and finds they call unequivocally for freedom:

"The divine liberation of the oppressed from slavery is the central theological concept in the black spirituals." Biblical images appear repeatedly: Moses and the Exodus, Daniel in the lion's den, the river Jordan, the Promised Land, the land of milk and honey. Black slaves wanted freedom from bondage, but freedom was not forthcoming, so they sought freedom from bondage and freedom in bondage. To achieve a sense of dignity is a triumph for the oppressed. Yet, for the black in bondage, the slender hope for freedom was not enough to sustain a sense of dignity; that power lay elsewhere. The question that remains is, How did they claim freedom in bondage? How did they nurture their self-esteem? The answer to these questions lies in their religion: "The essence of ante-bellum black religion was the emphasis on the somebodiness of black slaves."[12] How could they affirm themselves? How could they experience this sense of being somebody? How could they seize control of their lives? Nat Turner rebelled; others fled on the underground railroad; but the vast majority had to bow to their masters and risk internalizing the image of the docile slave. They had to hide their dignity to survive.

The slave's struggle was a struggle to affirm "both his being and his being-in-community, for the two are inseparable." Remaining in community was difficult; a mother, father, or child could be torn away at any moment. Family was at best a tentative state for the slave and always occasioned the most painful loss; "that was why most of the slave songs focus on going home."[13] Home was the affirmation of the need for community whether in this life or the next. The meaning of freedom was as much corporate as it was individual. It meant more than individual liberty;

it meant the freedom to live in community, to have a
family.

Freedom is the central motif in black religion, but it is
not the center of black faith. In an essay entitled "Black
Church: Origin, History, Present Dilemmas," Preston N.
Williams concedes "the primacy of freedom and equality"
in the thoughts of the black people, but he insists that the
religious quest is broader.[14] Black religion must give a
reason for living even under the condition of slavery. In
this quest for meaning, freedom alone is not enough. Freedom is the means, not the end. Freedom drives toward
something. Unfortunately, the concept of freedom has
proved to be a stumbling block for many black theologians
in that it became the goal of religion.

in Black Theology. He points out that most black theologians have mistaken the object of faith in black religion.
Cecil Cone considers his brother James one of the misguided and asks him where his confessional commitment
lies: "Is it to the black religious experience, or to the black
power motif of liberation with a sidelong glance at the
black religious experience?" In overemphasizing liberation
James Cone is proclaiming a form of henotheism, making
a finite, sociopolitical experience the object of trust and
loyalty. But what is needed is a transcendent focus of
faith. Thus, Cecil Cone argues that the true focus of black
faith is the Almighty God and the conversion experience
that marks this encounter. This is an ecstatic experience
after which one places one's ultimate faith in God, and it is
as one of God's children that one is somebody. "The dignity of man is created by God."[15]

God is the central focus of black religion. It is to Him
that the slaves turned. On Him they relied, and in Him

they found solace. Freedom is a byproduct of the slaves' relationship to God, and this was the only relationship the master was powerless to sever. Their connection to Him ensured and affirmed their dignity. On the auction block and in death the slave triumphed because this freedom-in-bondage was essentially spiritual; it was a feeling, an inner knowledge and peace, and it was inviolable.

McClendon, after examining the life of Martin Luther King, Jr., comes to a similar conclusion about black religion. He focuses on three crises in King's life and finds that King prayed at these moments. He prayed not as a public utterance but as "the inner dialogues of a man whose last resource was not himself but God." Through the life of King, McClendon finds the essence of black religion to be *"a religious experience* engraved in spirituals and sermons and frenzy alike [that] *lies at the heart of that religion, and that experience* is an experience *of God and self as one."*[16] God is the center of black faith and spiritual freedom is the means to and the byproduct of the ecstatic experience of one's relationship to God.

It is important to note that in the black spirituals "statements about God are not theologically distinct from statements about Jesus Christ."[17] There is a distinction, but it is not a matter of theology. It is a matter of the experience of His presence.

> In the spirituals God is experienced as Almighty and Sovereign and is often removed from the day-to-day affairs of people. But Jesus is experienced as a comforter in time of trouble who is readily available and always at hand.[18]
>> "I'm a chile of God wid my soul set free,
>> For Christ hab bought my liberty."[19]

To know this gave the slave a freedom that bondage could not suppress. Knowing dignity through his connection to God and having the support of his brother Jesus, the slave met life. In this internal freedom, slaves found strength and confidence, and knew freedom would become the external reality as well. This was the source of black hope. Frederick Douglass, in his autobiography, describes this hope instilled in him by his chief religious instructor, who was known as Uncle Lawson:

> He fanned my already intense love of knowledge into a flame by assuring me that I was to be a useful man in the world. When I would say to him, "How can these things be? and What can I do?" his simple reply was, "Trust in the Lord." When I would tell him, "I am a slave, and a slave for life, how can I do anything?" he would quietly answer, "The Lord can make you free, my dear; all things are possible with Him; only have faith in God. 'Ask, and it shall be given you.' If you want liberty, ask the Lord for it in faith, and He will give it to you."
>
> Thus assured and thus cheered on under the inspiration of hope, I worked and prayed with a light heart, believing that my life was under the guidance of a wisdom higher than my own. With all other blessings sought at the mercy seat, I always prayed that God would, of His great mercy, and in His own good time, deliver me from my bondage.[20]

In the experience described in this passage, and in every slave that yearned for freedom Christianity met an African world view which set a tone of strength and faith.

The continued oppression of black Americans as a group has sustained this drive toward freedom in our age. But it is only in our age that the always present tension between this-worldly and other-worldly religion has become more pronounced. Many accuse the church of having become other-worldly and offering members mere compensation for their sufferings, but Cecil Cone insists that these critics

fail to grasp the meaning of the other-worldly language in the black religious experience. In the black religious experience the talk about heaven, God and freedom has a double meaning. While it is true that it refers to life after death, it also refers to life here and now, the future in this life. That is, God through his gift of grace has allowed his people to experience a "foretaste of glory divine." This enables them to endure oppression and gives them the necessary strength and insight to participate with the divine in the final destruction of oppression here on earth.[21]

Despite the intended "double meaning" of this other-worldly language, and perhaps because of it, there is an undeniable tension between a this-worldly and an other-worldly focus. There is an ebb and flow in which other-worldly concerns have often surged forward. The surge of other-worldly religion came as a reaction to further disillusionment. For the slaves the millennium was heralded with the Emancipation Proclamation, established in Reconstruction, and killed at the hands of Jim Crow. The former slave now had to struggle for the political freedom that was supposedly already won. The goal of freedom was less tangible than before but no less elusive, and the double meaning of freedom spoken from the pulpit became more ambiguous. As the fight for political freedom was taken up by secular organizations, the black church became increasingly de-radicalized. In later years, according to Gayraud Wilmore in *Black Religion and Black Radicalism*, the church was caught between those embittered by an "unjust God" and those who considered themselves above the black preacher. Under fire from two sides, the church retreated.

> Their churches turned inward to spiritual needs of a deprived and oppressed people who found emotional release from the victimization of the white world in the ritual and organizational effervescence of Black church life.[22]

The spiritual freedom that once gave the slave strength to carry on in bondage was now so altered that it simply invited the freed man and woman to escape this worldly plight. When participation in this world was no longer of concern, political freedom became inconsequential. Still, the drive toward freedom, if suspended for a time, remained. It reemerges today in Jesse Jackson's litany "I am somebody," which harkened back to the slaves' struggle to affirm their dignity in the 1950s. It reappeared in Martin Luther King, Jr., the black Moses who went to the mountain top and saw the Promised Land. To inspire those in the civil rights movement he drew on the rich biblical tradition and particularly upon Exodus. From the Old Testament, he called forth the story of God and man acting in tandem upon history. The black quest for freedom had not died, it had merely been smoldering.

When the hope for political freedom was rekindled in the black soul, it was due in no small part to the rise of the democratic faith in the United States. In a sermon entitled "The Death of Evil Upon the Seashore," Martin Luther King, Jr., intertwined the images of the biblical and American traditions. He presented Thomas Jefferson as a man tortured by the unbearable paradox of slavery in the midst of freedom. He evoked the story of the Afro-American, whose singular experience ties him or her to this country.[23]

The black experience in America has been penetrated by the American ideal of a free democracy and in turn has influenced that ideal. Blacks fought in the War of Independence and every other American war. Once freed, they understood that the heritage of America was their heritage. They took their seats in the Reconstruction legislatures. When ejected, they fought their way back into the political system. The Back-to-Africa schemes did not win them. DuBois understood that blacks participated in the foundation of this country, and that from their labor and their lives slaves unwillingly sustained the nation as it grew. But beyond this he found that the black American had given an even greater gift:

> One cannot think of democracy in America or in the modern world without reference to the American Negro. The democracy established in America in the eighteenth century was not, and was not designed to be, a democracy of the masses of men and it was thus singularly easy for people to fail to see the incongruity of democracy and slavery. It was the Negro himself who forced the consideration of this incongruity, who made emancipation inevitable and made the idea of a democracy including men of all races and colors.[24]

The black American has had a hidden symbiotic relationship with this basic American ideal. Knowledge of this American ideal gave the slave and later the sharecropper and the slum dweller grounds for hope, and this hope, transformed into action, has put the American democratic faith to one of its greatest tests. When King spoke the words "I have a dream" during the march on Washington, he united a biblical vision with the American ideal to proclaim the coming fulfillment of the American faith.

> I have a dream that one day this nation will rise up and live out the true meaning of its creed: We hold these truths to be self-evident, that all men are created equal.[25]

In summary, freedom has been and is the dominant image in the black American experience. But in the context of black religion, freedom is the means, not the end; the object of faith in black religion is God. Black religion agrees with H. Richard Niebuhr's description of the churches of the disinherited. The ecstatic spiritual rapport with God, the reliance upon His grace, the absence of complex doctrines and creeds, and corporate redemption in the salvation of the black people are all elements of black religion. In our time one can see the waning of these characteristics, and the lives of Ethelred Brown and Lewis McGee dramatize this transformation in the black culture.

In black religion freedom emerges as a three-dimensional experience. Spiritual freedom has primacy, but must hold this-worldly and other-worldly concerns in equilibrium. When other-worldly concern is paramount, black religion plunges into escapism, and when this-worldly concern dominates, God, the source of power, is forgotten. Increasingly in the modern world, political freedom has vied with spiritual freedom for the loyalty of black people, and the American democratic faith strengthens the appeal of political freedom as an object of faith. Finally, intellectual freedom, while always present and active in its aesthetic form, is exercised primarily in the service of the other two.

Let us now consider Unitarianism to see to what degree it fits Niebuhr's typology of a middle-class religion and to identify the dominant images in the literature of that tradition.

UNITARIANISM

I call that mind free which
masters the senses,
And which recognizes its own
reality and greatness.
WILLIAM ELLERY CHANNING
"Spiritual Freedom"
May 26, 1830

H. Richard Niebuhr points out that middle-class religions tend to be more philosophical, abstract, and formal than those of the disinherited; Unitarianism is an example of this tendency. In searching the Unitarian literature, I found a dearth of images. No grand story of suffering emerges; rather, there are philosophical discourses, lifeless histories, and theological sermons. But in examining those seemingly lifeless histories, I found the images lying in plain sight. I was led to them by an exploration of the dominant concepts of Unitarianism, and it is there that I will begin.

Earl Morse Wilbur, in his two-volume history of Unitarianism, identifies three guiding principles in the liberal faith: complete intellectual freedom, reason, and tolerance. The three are interdependent, each relying on the others to sustain it; but of the three, intellectual freedom evokes the strongest response. Individuals had reason, they never really understood tolerance, but they struggled for a greater freedom of mind: freedom to exercise their reason, freedom to seek the truth, freedom to declare that truth, and freedom to live within its realm. The dominant concept in the liberal church is this freedom, an intellectual freedom.

> I call that mind free which
> jealously guards its intellectual
> rights and powers,
> Which does not content itself with
> a passive or hereditary faith.

Freedom Moves West is the title of Charles Lyttle's history of the Western Unitarian Conference, in which he states that "freedom of thought, sovereignty of ethics [and] spiritual democracy" are the chief Unitarian principles, and in the American move west Unitarianism was first identified with the advance of intellectual culture. He describes the westward spread of Unitarianism and relates that the Western Conference stood stalwartly for intellectual freedom in religion against the theologically conservative and denominationally all-powerful New Englanders. In the past, intellectual freedom in the Unitarian church was not boundless, and its limits were gradually expanded. Lyttle writes in conclusion, "Free Religion . . . guard[ed] the mind of man from bondage. . . [The Unitarian task was and is] to go forth against authoritarianism in all its ominous forms political, economic, religious."[26] The freedom that is foremost in the heart of the Unitarian is the freedom of the mind, not of the body, for the enslavement they struggled against was intellectual and psychological,

not physical. Political freedom is practically an after-
thought for Unitarians; it is assumed.

> I call that mind free which
> protects itself against the
> usurpation of society.
> And which does not cower to
> human opinion.

To better understand the reason behind this Unitarian
attitude toward intellectual freedom, we should examine
the religious perspectives of the Unitarian's forebears.
Americans generally accept the myth that the original Puritans were driven out of England. This is not true. Their departure from England "was an act of will . . . They [went]
of their own accord" to establish "a city on a hill." They
went not to escape political oppression as much as to establish a community with a covenant—a model of God's
will. At its inception this community comprised free individuals. Members relied upon a limited reason in interpret-
ing and following God's Law, but were careful to avoid
imitating their contemporary Arminians, who were thought
to have gone too far in the "exaltation of human reason."[27] These early Puritans had no intention of tolerating
doctrines that varied from those of the Puritan elect. Indeed it was, as Sidney Mead asserts, only in adjusting to
the political and religious realities of colonial America that
they "placed their feet unwittingly on the road to religious
freedom. Thus, they came upon religious freedom not as
the cheerful givers their Lord is said to love, but grudgingly and of necessity." Religious freedom in America was a
compromise. It was not a tenet of any tradition save the

Baptist and the Quaker, and few people recited biblical passages justifying it. Little commitment was given to religious freedom as an active value as long as each denomination was left to go its own way. The individuals to whom it fell to make "sense theoretically out of the actual, practical situation which demanded religious freedom" were "the effectively powerful intellectual, social, and political leaders." They were rationalists who "gave it tangible form and legal structure."[28]

It is no wonder then that while there are intellectual concepts, Unitarianism lacks imagery. Finding little justification within the Bible (the deuteronomic writers were wholly intolerant of other religions), the concept of tolerance was articulated in philosophical and legal terms, as in the Statute of Virginia for Religious Freedom, written by Thomas Jefferson. Religious freedom was part and parcel of the freedom of the mind the Enlightenment had glorified.

Americans may have accepted religious freedom grudgingly, but they felt little ambiguity about political and economic freedom. The colonists rose up when their economic and political freedom was threatened. The War of Independence reasserted that freedom, but its deeper meaning lapsed once again into the American subconscious. Jefferson, seeing this, wrote:

From the conclusion of this war we shall be going downhill. It will not be necessary to resort every moment to the people for support. They will be forgotten, therefore, and their rights disregarded. They will forget themselves but in the sole faculty of making money, and will never think of uniting to effect a due respect for their rights. The shackles, therefore,

which shall not be knocked off at the conclusion of
this war, will remain on us long, will be made heavier
and heavier, till our rights shall revive or expire in
a convulsion.[29]

To our credit, we have not gone only downhill. Blacks,
women, and union workers have all risen up and demanded
their rights, but each of these revolutions subsided after
the achievement of a higher standard of living. Each group
acquiesced as the members' stake in the status quo increased. People are most concerned with their freedom
when it is threatened or lost. At other times they quickly
turn to other pursuits. They plunge into the exercise of
economic freedom, forgetting the cost at which that freedom was bought or the responsibility it entails. Freedom
becomes a byword for the quest after economic prosperity.

Religious freedom is of little concern for most Americans, since people have generally been left to believe as
they choose. Because there is no state religion, many of the
battles that might have arisen for religious freedom have
instead been intradenominational. This was particularly true
for the Unitarian movement, in which religious freedom
and complete intellectual freedom became synonymous.

> I call the mind free which
> resists the bondage of habit,
> Which does not mechanically copy
> the past, nor live on its old
> virtues.

Complete intellectual freedom for William Ellery Channing is "resisting the bondage" of biblical literalism. His
concept of freedom is discursive and abstract or, as indi-

cated in his "Baltimore Address," left as an assumption
upon which the case for Unitarian Christianity is stated.
Ralph Waldo Emerson, in his "Divinity School Address,"
laces his discourse with pastoral and heavenly images, but
in calling for a new spiritual freedom he is already going
beyond intellectual freedom. In claiming God's immanent
presence, he is not mechanically copying the past, but
breaking new ground for intellectual and spiritual freedom.
For both of these men, freedom is more present in deed
than in word, more present in their persons than in any
concept they use.

> I call the mind free which sets
> no bounds to its love,
> Which, wherever they are seen,
> delights in virtue and sympathizes
> with suffering.[30]

Channing was concerned with freedom, both intellectual
and physical. He was in the forefront of the fight for ra-
tional religion, which implied a free mind, and for abolition, which demanded freedom for the slaves. It fell to
Theodore Parker to eloquently and radically call for total
human freedom. His sermon entitled "The Transient and
Permanent in Christinity" pushed what was then the acceptable boundary for freedom of religious thought to its
limits. Elsewhere, his dramatic tale of sitting up nights
writing his sermons with a gun on his desk and a sword at
his side so that he might protect the runaway slaves he
harbored in his home left no doubt about how highly he
prized freedom. Parker was not alone, but he was part of a
small minority who passionately fought against slavery and
for intellectual freedom.

The desire for freedom from human bondage is expressed in the current Unitarian hymnal, *Hymns for the Celebration of Life:*

> Let all who live in freedom, won by sacrifice of others,
> Be untiring in the task begun till everyone on earth
> is free.[31]

The vast majority of Unitarian hymns address the question of spiritual and intellectual freedom, as in Samuel Longfellow's "O Life That Maketh All Things New":

> One in the freedom of the truth,
> One in the joy of paths untrod,
> One in the soul's perennial youth
> One in the larger thought of God.[32]

In a similar manner, Charles Lyttle's lyric entitled "Church of the Free Spirit" focuses on the concepts of Truth, Good, and Agape:

> Bring, O Past, your honor; bring, O Time, your harvest,
> Golden sheaves of hallowed lives and minds by Truth
>   made free;
> Come, you faithful spirits, builder of this temple:
> "To Holiness, to Love and Liberty."[33]

These and other hymns tend to extol abstract human virtues. As Unitarians, we pay lip service to a spirituality we are hard pressed to find in our congregations. We also honor God, our forebears, and occasionally Jesus. We celebrate life. When we want concrete imagery, we evoke nature—her seasons, woods, and oceans. We praise the heavens—its stars, sun, and moon. We rarely turn to the

Bible, which is not surprising, since the Exodus was not primarily about intellectual freedom and Eve's use of freedom in the Garden of Eden is viewed as the cause of original sin. Jesus did not proclaim an end to intellectual oppression; he used his freedom to reinterpret the Law. Intellectual freedom was not his foremost concern; rather, a new social order and spiritual rebirth were his primary concerns. We honor him, not because he proclaimed intellectual freedom, but because he led a moral life. Religious liberals count him among our prophets because, as H. Richard Niebuhr points out, our self-sufficiency makes us task- and achievement-oriented, and we therefore need Jesus as an example to follow rather than as a comforter to lean on.

The call for intellectual freedom is simply not the central message of the Bible; it is at best found implicitly. It was probably the least of the concerns of biblical authors or of the many audiences addressed. More often these people were seeking answers to basic questions of existence. They were trying to preserve a community identity, assert their right to be, understand their enslavement, discover meaning in life, and overcome the fear of death. At most, intellectual freedom played a supportive role, only to be suppressed when it confronted the shibboleths of a tradition.

The typology of freedom—spiritual, political, and intellectual—that we found in black religion is reversed in the Unitarian faith. Intellectual freedom is foremost. The men and women who have pushed beyond the framework for belief in their religious communities are representative of the life that is fulfilled through intellectual freedom: Francis David debating at the Diet of Torda; Joseph

Priestley fleeing Manchester; Theodore Parker ostracized by almost every minister in Boston; the religious radicals of the Reformation, Michael Servetus and Francis David pursued that freedom at the cost of liberty and life. The political freedom upon which the freedom of speech depends is second in importance, and spiritual freedom is the Unitarian stepchild. Spiritual freedom is not disregarded—Emerson was its eloquent advocate—but it has rarely emerged as the cutting edge of the movement.

The great heroes in the Unitarian tradition are individuals who merge freedom's three dimensions in their lives and suffered because of their loyalty to these principles. Theodore Parker, as an advocate of the free mind, an abolitionist, and a transcendentalist, is a model of this union. Others uphold intellectual and political freedom. Priestley was attacked not only for his religion but also for his support of the French Revolution. In John Haynes Holmes, intellectual freedom and social concern were inextricable. Holmes, a pacifist and a socialist, helped to found the National Association for the Advancement of Colored People and the American Civil Liberties Union. The close tie between the intellectual and the political is also seen in A. Powell Davies, who extolled democracy over both communism and McCarthyism.

This last hero, A. Powell Davies, brings the imagery of the American democratic faith to bear upon his testimony. In *Man's Vast Future: A Definition of Democracy* he appeals to images of the American and French revolutions, of Justice Holmes, of Abraham Lincoln, and of that government of, by, and for the people.[34] Indeed, the foundation of this nation was an exercise of this dual freedom of the intellect and politics. The Constitution was a creation of the intellect, and its establishment an act of power. Some of the Unitarian's religious forebears were instrumental in the founding of the United States; thus, the Unitarian's connection with the ideal and images of American democracy is deep. The Unitarian has resources that address freedom on its most inclusive levels, but the predominant vision of freedom in the Unitarian eye is that of the individual mind. Niebuhr, in his description of middle-class religion, offers a penetrating analysis of this:

> The religious ethics of the middle class is marked throughout by this characteristic of individualism . . . Such an ethics is capable of producing a real heroism of self-discipline and, in its insistence on personal responsibility, the courage of resistance to the authority of state and church when these conflict with the imperatives of individual conscience. But this morality is incapable of developing a hopeful passion for social justice. Its martyrs die for liberty not for fraternity and equality; its saints are patrons of individual enterprise in religion, politics, and economics, not the great benefactors of mankind or the heralds of brotherhood.[35]

Niebuhr's charge is captured in the title of Vincent Silliman's popular hymn "Faith of the Free." There is an ambiguity hidden in these words. Is Unitarianism the "faith of the free," meaning the church of the free—that is, the church that celebrates the free mind and individual conscience? Or is Unitarianism the faith *of those who are* free— that is, those who are both politically free and free from economic oppression, such as the middle class. In the double meaning of the hymn's title, "Faith of the Free," and in its lyrics, this hymn epitomizes the Unitarian image of freedom:

Faith of the larger liberty
Source of the light expanding,
Law of the church that we shall be,
Old bondage not withstanding;
Faith of the free! By thee we live—
By all thou givest and shall give
Our loyalty commanding.

Heroes of faith in every age,
Farseeing, self-denying,
Wrought an increasing heritage,
Monarch and priest defying.
Faith of the free! In thy dear name
The costly heritage we claim:
Their living and their dying.

Faith for the people everywhere,
Whatever their oppression,
Of all who make the world more fair,
Living their faith's confession:
Faith of the free! What e'er our plight,
Thy law, thy liberty, thy light
Shall be our blest possession.[36]

Niebuhr's description of the churches of the middle class seems applicable to Unitarianism. His "real heroism of self-discipline" is echoed in the phrase "Heroes of faith in every age,/Farseeing, self-denying." His idea of "the courage of resistance to the authority of state and church" appears as "Wrought an increasing heritage/Monarch and priest defying." Niebuhr claims that for the middle class, striving, rather than grace, predominates. The "faith of the free" is something "we live" and "we claim"; it is "our blest possession." It is not so much a gift as a goal we strive toward. The individualistic character of the middle class permeates Unitarianism.

This conclusion is also supported by Robert L'H. Miller's study "The Religious Value System of Unitarian Universalists." Using the Rakeach Value Survey, Miller finds that the Unitarian Universalist's "orientation [is] towards competence rather than morality and stresses personal realization, individual self-fulfillment, and self-actualization."[37] In this survey, as one would expect, freedom is ranked significantly higher than equality, and Unitarian Universalists rank equality lower than any of the other religious groups surveyed. Salvation, a primary expectation of the disinherited, "comes close to being a disvalue for Unitarian Universalists."[38] It is not surprising that the values of the Unitarians correlate most closely with the values of the top income level of the other religious groups measured and correlate least with the values of those in the lowest income level.

When we compare the dimensions of freedom in black religion and Unitarianism, we see that their order is reversed. Intellectual freedom dominates in liberal religion and holds only a limited, supportive role in black religion. Spiritual freedom is paramount in black religion, but leads to an ecstatic other-worldly escapism when it is not balanced by other concerns. Intellectual freedom, when it is overemphasized in Unitarianism, dissolves into dissociated intellectualism and esoteric escapism. In neither of these situations are the active qualities of the spiritual and the intellectual brought to bear upon the reality of this world. Political freedom often emerges as a strong force in both traditions. In Unitarianism political concerns occasionally take over at the expense of free dialogue, and in the black tradition political concerns have often meant forsaking God and church. In both traditions a small group of people has managed to hold these freedoms in symbiotic relationship. Finally, spirituality in both Unitarianism and black religion is manifested in a sense of connectedness. In black religion this connectedness is the source of an integrity and involves a vertical connection to God and a horizontal link with community and family. In Unitarianism this connectedness is more immanent, and its end is to lift individuals from their separation from the world. Herein, the individual is freed from the sense of isolation that middle-class life generates.

The stories that lie before us are those of Egbert Ethelred Brown and Lewis Allen McGee, two men reared in the black religious tradition who embraced Unitarianism and strove to propagate it in the black community. Their experiences and fate bear witness to the meeting of these two diverse traditions.

Egbert Ethelred Brown

Chapter Two

A Dream Aborted: Egbert Ethelred Brown in Jamaica and Harlem

Both divisions within the liberal religious tradition, the Unitarians and the Universalists, had tenuous relationships with the black community. The life of Egbert Ethelred Brown represents only one story of a struggle to overcome the separation between blacks and followers of the liberal faith.

In 1889 Joseph H. Jordan (1842–1901), a black convert to Universalism, established a church in West Norfolk, Virginia, and later his associate, Thomas E. Wise, organized a second mission in the city of Suffolk. The leadership of this church fell in 1904 to Joseph Fletcher Jordan (1863–1929), who was not related to the first Jordan. The second Jordan studied at St. Lawrence Theological School during the 1903–1904 academic year and then took up his duties in Virginia only to find that Wise had returned to Methodism. There were "fifty families in [Jordan's] parish, twenty-three church members [and] a sunday school of 44." Besides the church, he operated a school with 129 pupils and published a monthly paper called *The Colored Universalist*.[1] After Joseph F. Jordan died, the church, despite efforts to keep it going, finally closed.[2] His daughter, Annie B. Willis, however, had great success with the

31

Mission School, and the Universalists continued to support it into the 1960s; it existed until recently as the Jordan Neighborhood House. The more explicitly Christian and spiritual tendencies in Universalism evoked quite a different response from the black community than that evoked by Unitarianism, but still did not bridge the chasm that separated the liberal faith and the black community.

The Universalists, like the Unitarians, were no more outspoken about race than were any other white Christians, but there were exceptional Universalist individuals. Benjamin Rush helped to found the organization of the Society for the Abolition of Slavery in 1790. He also helped finance and support the efforts of Richard Allen in 1793 to establish an African church in Philadelphia.[3] This movement later became the African Methodist Episcopal church (AME), the first of the black denominations. Other Universalists like Elhanan Winchester and later Adin Ballou spoke out against slavery.

The Unitarians were also well represented among the abolitionists through people like Theodore Parker, William Ellery Channing, and Samuel J. May, but not until May 1844, after years of interminable debate, was their association successfully badgered into passing a moderate antislavery resolution. Many influential Unitarians not only resisted this but also refused to open their churches to blacks. Indeed, Unitarians did not try to spread their message among blacks; their mission work was done through the Society for Propagating the Gospel among the Indians and Others in North America. This society, which was organized in 1787, administered funds for the benefit of "Indians and Colored people." It did not endeavor to spread liberal Christianity, but rather worked only in connection with established religious missions.[4] Apparently, Unitarians felt it was enough for nonwhite people to embrace Christian orthodoxy. The underlying paternalism in the Unitarian attitude toward blacks becomes even more apparent as one looks at the life of Ethelred Brown.

JAMAICA

Early in the year 1920 Ethelred Brown and his wife, Ella, boarded a steamer in Jamaica bound for New York City. Behind him that tropical island which had once been the hub of the slave trade and was even then covered with plantations worked by the poorly paid descendents of kidnapped Africans, Brown abandoned all hope of establishing a Unitarian mission. After eight years of struggle, his hope for a church lay broken. Debt pressed down on him, his children were living temporarily with their grandparents, and he was sailing for New York, seeking another chance to bring Unitarianism to the black community.

Egbert Ethelred Brown, born in Falmouth, Jamaica, in the British West Indies, on July 11, 1875, to James and Florence Brown, was the eldest of five children. When Ethelred later reflected upon the youthful inclinations that propelled him toward the ministry, he noted "a distinct recollection that as a child [he] liked to make speeches."[5] He recalled organizing "little services with his brothers and other youngsters."[6] He also remembered:

> There was, coincident with my childish experiments in making speeches, an abnormally religious temperament. In all other respects I think I was a normal boy, but at times I was seized by a religious fervor which I now know was abnormal. My favorite hymn was, "O Paradise 'tis weary waiting here."

I sang it often, and as I sang, my face was bathed
in tears. Why should a boy have chosen a hymn so
other-worldly?

This is a question Brown did not answer, but he did go
on to write, "I somewhat outgrew the abnormal religiousness of my youth."[7]

It was not always clear that Ethelred would enter the
ministry. "His parents and friends predicted for him a
place either in the pulpit or at the bar."[8] And in school,
Ethelred took on the role of prosecuting attorney in a
juvenile court. This led him to entertain the idea of becoming a lawyer, but his father, an auctioneer, was at the time
unable to finance his education. In later years his father's
greater prosperity enabled one of Ethelred's brothers to
become a lawyer, and another became the first black
canon in Jamaica. Ethelred did not have the advantages of
his younger brothers. In 1894 at the age of nineteen,
Brown placed third in an examination given throughout
the island for entrance into the civil service of Jamaica. In
1899 he was promoted to first clerk of the treasury, where
he worked until 1907, when on the eve of another promo-
tion he was suddenly dismissed. Brown wrote that his dismissal occurred under "peculiar circumstances," ones that
he called "tragic," "cataclysmic," and "providential." He
did not say exactly what happened, but his eldest daughter
recalls hearing her uncles speak of the incident among
themselves. According to them, Ethelred was sending his
wife to Kingston for singing lessons, supporting four children, and paying high rent. He had taken money from the
treasury with the intention of paying it back, but before
he could afford to do so, the funds were found to be miss-

ing. His father and brothers paid the debt. He lost his job, but was not prosecuted.[9] The dismissal precipitated a personal crisis. At the age of thirty-two Brown had been settled into his secure government position, and its sudden loss came to represent a turning point in his life, a point at which he reassessed his life direction and resolved to become a minister.

As Ethelred assessed his life, he addressed himself about his earlier response to a call to the ministry:

> You ought to have been in the ministry long ago. When your brother sailed for Africa [four years earlier] you knew then beyond doubt that you were called to the ministry, but you resisted the call because your position in the Civil Service was financially secure. Now God himself in his own way has deprived you of the security. Your duty is clear.

Ethelred Brown's decision to enter the ministry cannot be attributed to sibling rivalry or to capriciousness. Looking back, he could see the signs in his youthful character:

> I was an inquisitive youngster and a truthful child. I was disposed to ask questions. I remember very distinctly the question which I asked my teacher after the scripture lesson on the falling of the walls of Jericho. "Why," I asked, "did God waste so much time when he could have brought down the walls on the first day?" My teacher was horrified. So much for my inquisitiveness. From accounts I heard later in life I have come to the conclusion that as a child I told the truth instinctively, or if you prefer the term, automatically. These two characteristics—inquisitiveness and truthfulness—had much to do with the choice I ultimately made to enter the Unitarian ministry.

His was not a sudden turn to religion: He had been an active church member for most of his life, and he felt he had been "called." But his discovery of Unitarianism happened by chance one Easter Sunday.

> I was a choir boy of Montego Bay Episcopal Church when the first ray of light broke through my Trinitarianism. It was Easter Sunday. We did not as usual sing the Athanasian Creed: it was recited alternately by the priest and the congregation. The strangeness of the Trinitarian arithmetic struck me forcibly—so forcibly that I decided then and there to sever my connection with the church which enunciated so impossible a proposition.[10]

Brown's decision was followed almost immediately by his discovery of Unitarianism:

> That afternoon—mind you, that very Sunday afternoon—I visited my uncle and there on a table were the words The Lord our God is one God. It turned out to have been a copy of Channing's memorable sermon preached in Baltimore on the ordination of Jared Sparks. My uncle was a Unitarian, but he was not carried away with the idea of a possible youthful convert, and so it was only after much beseeching that he gave me the sermon. I took it home and read it and discovered that in America there were Christians who did not believe in the Athanasian Creed. A few days after my uncle sent me with a note to a physician, and in his study there was a library of Unitarian books including a hymn book which he gave me.[11]

This exposure to Unitarian literature proved to be the intellectual beginning for Brown.

> I followed up by reading other Unitarian literature and as a result I became a Unitarian without a church.

For some years I attended no church, and then on a Sunday morning in 1895 I was drafted to take the place of the sick organist of the Montego Bay Wesleyan Methodist Church. On that day I began four years of service as organist of that church. On my transfer to Spanish Town in 1899 I was placed in charge of the choir of the Wesleyan Church of that town. Thus for nearly twelve years I forgot my Unitarian theology as I engaged in these services as organist of two Trinitarian churches. Then came 1900—the year of decision . . . With that call came a very urgent and important question, namely this—into the ministry of which denomination should I enter? All the doubts and questionings which were lulled to rest during the years of my active service in the Wesleyan Methodist Church were re-awakened. The conviction deepened that I could not honestly be a Methodist minister. Circumstances very soon created a conflict and forced a decision.

The African Methodist Episcopal Church of America had recently started work in Jamaica. After many interviews I was persuaded by its resident Representative to apply for admission into the ministry of that church. I did; but I had not well posted my letter of application when my outraged conscience violently protested. Four days later another letter was posted, strangely, addressed—"To any Unitarian Minister in New York City," seeking information as to the possibility of entering the Unitarian ministry. That letter ultimately reached the Rev. George Badger, then Secretary of the Fellowship Committee of the American Unitarian Association who referred it to President Franklin Southworth of the Meadville Theological School.

The mail which brought a reply from the Bishop of the A.M.E. Church which was practically an acceptance, brought also a reply from President Southworth. The latter informed me that the school did not conduct a correspondence course, and that therefore I would have to come to Meadville. And that as there was no Unitarian Church in America for colored people, and that as white Unitarians required a white minister he was unable to predict what my future would be at the conclusion of my training. The issue was clear; the conflict was short, but sharp.

On the one hand was the acceptance into the ministry of one church with the opportunity to begin my ministry at once, and on the other hand there was the imperative of years of training away from home, with no certainty as to the future. I decided that I was not compelled to be a minister of religion at all; but if I *did* enter the ministry I was under moral and spiritual compulsion to be a minister only of that church in which I would be absolutely honest. I therefore withdrew my application to enter the ministry of the African Methodist Episcopal Church and continued my correspondence with President Southworth. That correspondence ended with my acceptance as a special two-year student of the Meadville Theological School.[12]

The practical problems that lay in the way of his getting to Meadville were formidable. Brown related that his letters requesting assistance from the American Unitarian Association (AUA) received encouraging responses, but one AUA official later wrote, "Strong effort was made to dissuade him because it seemed so uncertain whether or not he could ever find a parish, but against all counsel he went to Meadville."[13] Brown was receiving contradictory messages from America, and in these lie the first hint of the thirty-year battle with the AUA that was to follow.

Brown prepared to leave for the United States and in a *Christian Register* article he recalled the days before his departure. He had been given a present by Methodist friends.

"I cannot accept your present until I tell you the purpose of my visit to America. I go to a theological school to be prepared for the Unitarian ministry. And, in case some of you may not know what is the distinctive teaching of Unitarianism, I may say that a Unitarian is one who denies the doctrine of the Trinity and the deity of Jesus Christ." Thus in July 1908, at the close of a Christian Endeavor meeting in the Montego Bay Wesleyan Methodist Church did I briefly make what I believe was the first public Unitarian pronouncement in the Island of Jamaica. The candle of Unitarianism was lighted—lighted, I hope, never to be put out. But the words which lighted it fell like a bomb on the quiet community, and men and women were amazed at "this strange teaching." At once I felt the consequences of my act. I was forthwith forbidden to perform my duties as organist in the church where for thirteen years I had led its singing and from the pulpit of which for eight years I had preached. And, although a little band of Christian Endeavorers, led by the minister, did give me a present and a word of cheer and good-will on the eve of my departure, the present of the church was withheld and the prayers of the members were unuttered.[14]

This was only the first of the many trials Brown would face over the years. Given the obstacles he faced it is remarkable that he became a Unitarian minister at all. Brown's enrollment at Meadville meant that his wife and children had to depend financially on Brown's father and on the Brooks Fellowship he received to assist them while he was away.

That it would require tenacity for Brown to complete his course of study is obvious from his first effort to get to Meadville:

In August 1908 I sailed on a fruit boat from Montego
Bay, my home town, for Baltimore, Maryland, intend-
ing to proceed from Baltimore to Richmond, Virginia,
to serve as an accountant for a colored building con-
tractor until the end of September when I would leave
his employ to enter the Meadville Theological School.
Such was my intention, but thus it was not to be.
Having secured my appointment as an accountant
before entering America, and having so informed
Immigration officials, I was declared a contracted
alien and was ordered deported. After an absence of
two weeks I was again in Montego Bay, no longer a
Wesleyan Methodist but a self-declared Unitarian.

I was back in Montego Bay to receive in full the
results of my apostasy. Of all that I suffered in those
early days I dare not write.

Under the law I could not return to America until
the expiration of one year after deportation. During
the year of waiting I established a Unitarian Lay Center in Montego Bay. Open air meetings were held at
which the gospel of Unitarianism was preached. (This
was done amidst a storm of pulpit criticism and newspaper controversy.) September 1909 arrived. My
passage for my second trip to Meadville by way of
New York was booked. Again I was disappointed. My
father who had promised to finance my passage withdrew his promise at the eleventh hour. I was booked
to sail on Tuesday. On Saturday evening I said good-
bye to my fellow clerks, but to the surprise of all I
was at my desk on Monday morning. The boat that
was to have taken me to America took a letter to
President Southworth explaining my second failure
to present myself at Meadville.

Two failures were not enough to kill my desire to
go to Meadville. My employer who flattered me by
his determination to keep me from going to America
and who influenced my father to refuse to aid me in-

creased my salary. I saved the increase and awaited
September 1910.

The third attempt to enter Meadville was successful. I arrived at last, and in September 1910 I was duly
enrolled as a special student of the school. The two
years which I spent at Meadville were years that I shall
ever remember. The happy days of genuine comrade-
ship will ever remain as a pleasant memory.[15]

Ethelred Brown became the seventh black to attend Meadville. The first, Alfred Amos Williams, an AME minister who
enrolled at Meadville in 1870, preceded him by forty years.[16]

Brown was not the first Meadville student to be considered a candidate to carry the message of liberal Christianity to the black community. In 1903 Don Speed Smith
Goodloe entered Meadville, and President Franklin Southworth held him in high regard. "He inspires me with quite
unusual confidence," he wrote. Southworth's hope was
that Goodloe would consent to mission work among his
people. Meadville's president seemed committed to this
and in the same letter continued, "I believe myself that
liberal Christianity has a mission to the blacks, whether it
is labelled Unitarian or not, and I want Meadville to help in
solving the race problem."[17] Meadville made a contribution
to solving this problem, but not in the way Southworth
had hoped. It appears that between the impossibility of
Goodloe's ministering to a Unitarian church, the improb-
ability of a liberal mission to blacks succeeding, the urgent
need to find a job in order to support his wife and three
children, and perhaps a lack of inclination toward the ministry on Goodloe's part, Goodloe did not ultimately enter
the Unitarian ministry.[18] In 1906 Goodloe simultaneously
graduated from Meadville and received an A.B. from Alle-

gheny College. He went on to make his mark in the field of education, becoming the first principal of Maryland State Normal School No. 3,[19] now Bowie State College.

The tone for Brown's stay at Meadville was set by Southworth, whose own commitment to "solving the race problem" was evident in the number of black students who attended the school during his tenure and the support he gave Goodloe and later Brown. Brown was unique because he was the first black student to be an avowed Unitarian, and thus Meadville was a haven for him. There, as a Unitarian, he was only one among many. His course work proceeded well, and he found the intellectual life stimulating. He even recalled feeling that he never experienced prejudice there. Jokingly, he once wrote that at Meadville there was discrimination in his favor: Other students shoveled snow, but he was excused from that task. But people were nevertheless influenced by racial stereotypes. On one occasion when Brown did something extraordinarily well, someone said to him, "You must have some white blood in you."[20] Still, this was a special time for Brown, and he later referred to those days as an "inspiring memory" that sustained him through the disappointments and disillusionments he later faced.

In a deceptive way Ethelred Brown happened upon Unitarianism at the right time. The vitality Samuel A. Eliot brought to the presidency of the American Unitarian Association was moving the denomination forward. Eliot's own early experience with missions in the Northwest and his successful ministry in Denver were the foundation upon which he proclaimed the AUA "a missionary Association."[21] It was natural that Brown's hopes and visions were caught up in the spirit of the Eliot administration.

One can well imagine the dreams that Ethelred and his fellow students envisioned and the high hopes they held for their ministries. Sadly, Brown would later lament that the officials of the American Unitarian Association were not like the men he had known at Meadville.

In June 1912 the Meadville *Quarterly Bulletin* reported on "a service of unusual interest" when, acting for the small Unitarian group in Montego Bay, the school ordained Brown.[22] Of this event and of his return home Brown wrote:

With befitting and imposing ceremony I was ordained a Unitarian Minister in the Meadville Unitarian Church and solemnly "set apart" to do the work of a Unitarian missionary. After visiting a few of the larger Unitarian Churches in this country and presenting my cause, and after lodging with President Southworth, who consented to act as treasurer of the "Jamaica Building Fund," all the money collected from these churches, I sailed in July 1912 with the hopes born from association with men of vision and missionary enthusiasm for my homeland, and immediately after arrival in the small town of Montego Bay, began my work as a Unitarian Missionary.[23]

In April of the next year the association sent a retired minister, the Reverend Hilary Bygrave, to Jamaica to evaluate the situation, for besides the mission in Montego Bay, another group had gathered in Alexandria. In his report Bygrave occasionally reveals an important awareness of the circumstances under which Brown worked as well as his own racial attitude. Bygrave's report on the Jamaican movement was the single most comprehensive document on this subject available to the association's directors and became the main basis for their later recommendations:

Montego Bay has a population of some 7000 inhabitants, the vast proportion of the people here, as at Kingston and everywhere else, being colored, the shades varying from absolute blackness to a whiteness indistinguishable from the English or American type.

The Rev. E. E. Brown is pronouncedly black, which is somewhat of a handicap to him in his work, since those of his race who are fortunate enough to approach absolute whiteness are too proud *"to sit under"* any minister save *"a white gentleman."* He is fairly well educated, seems endowed with tact and great common sense, and is a speaker of considerable eloquence and force.

I think it is matter for regret that on his return to Jamaica from the Meadville Theological School Mr. Brown did not begin his work at Kingston, where his opportunity would have been ten times larger. [The population of Kingston was about 70,000.] But he has struck his roots in Montego Bay, which is moreover his native place. Here he was born and brought up, and here the greater part of his life has been spent. I am happy to report that after careful investigation, there is no blot or stain upon his record or character. Like other prophets, like our Master himself, he suffers from the fact that one's native place is none too eager to honor native talent . . .

From the American and British & Foreign Unitarian Associations Mr. Brown receives five hundred dollars per annum. He earns a like amount yearly, by serving in some clerical capacity in one of the principal commercial houses, under the control of some Jewish gentlemen, who have sympathy for him and for the Unitarian cause.

So far as the establishing of a Unitarian Church is concerned, Mr. Brown has not proceeded *very far*, nor is likely to under present conditions. The Sunday gathering, and all other meetings, are held in his house, and number from 10 to 25 people. Mrs. Brown conducts a small Sunday School, furnishing five children of her own. As opportunity and means allow Mr. Brown gives "a lecture" on some week evening in the Town Hall, when he usually has a large audience.

On Sunday afternoon April 13th I preached in the Town Hall to about 60 people, and again in the evening to fully 300. On the following Monday and Tuesday evenings I spoke for an hour on each occasion to quite 300 people, and on each occasion another hour was spent in answering questions, which I had invited from the floor. In every case the major part of the audience was composed of *males*, and the larger proportion of them were young men. Some of the questions put to me were foolish enough from the Unitarian point of view, but on the other hand, many of them were eminently sensible and searching, indicating a remarkable degree of intelligence and up-to-dateness in recent lines of thought in science, philosophy, and religion.

. . . I took it for granted that I was voicing the sentiment of the American and British & Foreign Unitarian Associations when I said to Mr. Brown and Mr. Walker [Walker had gathered the group in Alexandria.] . . . with a great deal of positiveness, that no more Unitarian money would flow into Jamaica—other than what was now being sent—until the infant cause at Montego Bay was on surer and stronger footing.

Mr. Brown and his friends succeeded in convincing me that the one thing necessary to their making good in the community was a modest place of worship. About eighteen hundred, or at most two thousand dollars would provide a building of sufficient size for this purpose, over and above the price of land; and for that I think there is a sum more than sufficient in the hands of the President of the Meadville Theological School.

Had the two Associations had any adequate knowledge of the social and religious conditions of Jamaica

I think they might well have hesitated before commissioning Mr. Brown to plant our flag there. But to drop, or curtail the work there at the present time, would cause shame and confusion to Mr. Brown, and would make the Unitarian name a scoff and by-word in Jamaica.

If we want to do a bit of genuine humanitarian work for a quite intelligent class of distinctively colored people, seventy-five years removed from slavery, but still quite poorly paid in the matter of wage, with no thought of ever getting anything but love and respect in return, I urge that in some way, the cause there be given this further impetus to a more assured success.

. . . I should suggest that the united grant made by the two Associations should be lessened yearly for a period of three years, ceasing entirely at the close of the third year . . .

In regard to Mr. Walker I make no recommendations, not that he is not entirely worthy so far as I could discover, but from the simple fact that his lot is cast in a much smaller place than Montego Bay. Alexandria is 30 miles from the railway . . . Mr. Walker took the trouble to come to Montego Bay to attend our meetings there. He came evidently hoping that I could ordain him to the Unitarian ministry and promise him aid toward the construction of a place of meeting. I told him it was not in my power to do either, and tried to make him see the facts as I saw them, and urged him to use his strength and abilities in efforts looking toward the social uplift of his race as well as in the spread of the Unitarian faith. I laid great emphasis on this phase of work in conversation with Mr. Brown and I trust that the proper official will strongly impress upon him that he must make good along some line of social effort or uplift as well as in the matter of gathering a congregation of Unitarian believing souls.

In spite of the fact that Jamaica is celebrated for its rum, very little of which by the way stays on the Island, intoxication would not seem to be a very prevailing vice. So far as I could see the native population are quite sober people. Sexual irregularities, nay sexual excesses and predial larceny [the theft of land] are the great vices of the people.

If this report should come to the notice of any members of our household of faith, who are as much, or even more interested in social uplift effort than they are in our distinctively religious work, I trust they may feel moved to send some contribution to me or to Mr. Foote to aid this spirited young man in his work.[24]

There are ambiguities in the position Bygrave took. He did not find the prospects in Jamaica promising and thought it unfortunate that Brown was allowed to take up this mission at all. He advised that it be viewed, not as a religious endeavor, but as a "genuine humanitarian work" for "the social uplift" of the Negro race. Still, he held out some hope for the mission by offering to accept contributions for Brown, and he said he was convinced of the importance of building a house of worship. Yet he recommended "that the united grant made by the two Associations should be lessened yearly for a period of three years," and stopped at the end of that period.

Given the mixed nature of Bygrave's report, it is difficult to understand how Brown could have written Bygrave in June 1913, requesting him to present Brown's case before the churches of Boston. Yet Brown wrote:

In the face of your report and your strong recommendations I make bold to ask you for the sake of our work to arrange to do this. Your word will mean a good deal.

He went on to plead for the recognition of the uniqueness of his circumstances. He called the work he was engaged in an "experiment" and "an exceptional child," and he concluded the letter with a surprising request:

> Why has your report not been published? Can't you send a few lines to the Register?[25]

Brown made a great deal of Bygrave's report, and, as a prolific letter writer, probably persisted in writing Bygrave. In a letter written to Samuel Eliot two years later, Bygrave made a point of saying that he was avoiding Brown, who was visiting the United States and petitioning the association for further support. Moreover, Brown was apparently claiming Bygrave's unqualified support for his mission, leading Bygrave to advise Eliot that to the best of his recollection he had not given an "unqualified approval of him and his work." Bygrave recalls rather that he recommended that Eliot

> *drop it*, unless you are prepared to whole-heartedly permanently support the first and only Negro church in the world, since Mr. B being coal black himself could not hope to secure the cooperation of white people, and what was sadder still not even the *presence* of the whiter people *of his own race*.[26]

This exchange reveals an important element in Brown's character: He heard and saw what he wanted, and often that did not correspond with reality but rather reflected his strongly held hopes. When he wanted the mission in Jamaica to succeed, it was expedient to claim Bygrave's full support. But a decade later when he was settled in Harlem, he wrote of Bygrave, "His report was not enthusiastic, and yet he recommended the building at once in Montego

Bay of a $3,000 church."[27] Because of Brown's willful-
ness, the officers of the association found it extremely
difficult to communicate with him, and as time passed,
tensions between Brown and the association mounted.

Brown's account of what occurred in the years following Bygrave's report shows that the report only signaled
the beginning of the controversy between Brown and the
American Unitarian Association:

> I very soon learned that the men who directed the af-
> fairs of the AUA were not like the men at Meadville
> . . . They were "business" men. I worked in Montego
> Bay for two years and was transferred by the AUA to
> the City of Kingston, the metropolis of the island of
> Jamaica. After working in this city for only 18
> months, and at the very moment when all Jamaica
> was being stirred by a newspaper controversy which
> was then proceeding in the leading city paper, and
> when we were actually using the money collected by
> me in America to build a church on a lot of land do-
> nated to us, to the surprise of all Jamaica, by the son
> of the Episcopal Bishop of the island, the AUA sud-
> denly withdrew its grant on the grounds that results
> were not satisfactory.[28]

The question was, Satisfactory for whom? What Brown
saw as a success, his reluctant benefactors, the American
Unitarian Association and the British and Foreign Unitarian Association (B & FUA), perceived as a waste of their
resources. But their withdrawal was hardly sudden; Brown
could have seen the handwriting on the wall. The initial
three-year commitment from both the British and Foreign
Unitarian Association and the American Unitarian Association had ended. The B & FUA found the whole venture
unwarranted and Brown "not the type of man to entrust

with the organization and control of a Unitarian Church. He acted again and again from impulse and involved himself again and again in financial and other difficulties."[29] After terminating their aid in January 1914, the associations did not renew their grant. Meanwhile, Brown pressed on with his efforts to win the support of the AUA:

> I protested, I appealed, I reminded the Association that when the work was being carried on in the small town of Montego Bay with not one quarter of the possibilities of the large city of Kingston, the Rev. Hilary Bygrave, the official investigator of the Association wrote in 1913—"To drop or curtail the work at the present time would be to cause shame and confusion to Mr. Brown, and would make the Unitarian name a scoff and a by-word in Jamaica." All was of no avail, and on November 3, 1915 I received a letter from Dr. Samuel Eliot, then President of the Association, informing me of the action of the Board. I quote a paragraph from that letter: "While I grieve for the failure of the enterprise into which you have thrown yourself with such complete self-forgetfulness, I am even more distressed by the conditions which must immediately confront you. Our last paragraph on your salary has gone to you and I know that the financial conditions must be very difficult for you to face. If I remember rightly you have had some experience as an accountant and you will probably be able to secure employment and provide for the wants of your family. This, however, may take you a little time. I shall therefore ask you to accept an additional check of $100 which goes to you unofficially to help you while you are discovering new means of supporting yourself and your family. I beg you understand that those of us who have known of your work have fully appreciated the spirit in which it was undertaken and the zeal with which it has been conducted."

Dr. Eliot imagined that one setback terrible as it was could destroy the faith of a man who made three trips across the ocean in order to get to Meadville and left a young wife and four children in order to be trained for his life's work. It did not. My life's work, Yes, that is what I conceive a minister's work to be—for life—for better or for worse until death.

As I said, however, at the moment I was stunned. My wife came to my rescue with a bright suggestion. "Take this $100," she said, "and go to Boston and speak to the Directors face to face." It was my only $100 but I made a trip of faith and late in November 1915 I sat in the head office of the American Unitarian Association and faced its president. I am bound to say that the interview was painful beyond description. I was surprised, disappointed, disillusioned as I faced a standard of judgment which declared that the failure or success of a religious venture was based on the number of members enrolled and the amount of dollars collected. Such intangible considerations as the emancipating power of our message and the evidence on all hands of the effects of its leavening influence weighed not at all. For the first time my faith trembled in the balance and I decided to remain in Boston and not return to Jamaica to face, in the words of Mr. Bygrave, my shame and confusion.

At this point the late Dr. Charles Wendte came on the scene. He called a meeting of the Unitarian ministers in and around Boston. The meeting was well attended, intensely interesting and remarkably revealing.[30]

Brown later summarized the results of this meeting:

The men by unanimous vote agreed to recommend the AUA to send me back to Jamaica. The fight was against Dr. Eliot . . . who surprised all present by his undisguised opposition to the work in Jamaica, an island of Negroes.[31]

Finally, Brown could conclude his narration of this trip on a positive note:

> Dr. Eliot who at first blamed me for my expensive and futile trip, at the close of this meeting tapped me on the shoulders and said—"A trip of faith, Mr. Brown, a trip of faith.[32]

I have cited at length Brown's description of these events, because the racial attitudes Brown encountered in Eliot and Louis C. Cornish, the secretary of the American Unitarian Association, posed very real obstacles for Brown: Their view of blacks was so limited that they never seriously believed that Unitarianism could be grasped by them. This attitude undermined Brown's mission from the outset. While Brown struggled to build greater support for his mission in Jamaica, the association's officers were questioning whether such a mission could ever succeed.

Brown's daughter, Dorice, once openly challenged the association's attitude with this raw assertion in a letter to the AUA: "So you seem to think we are some sort of savages."[33] Indeed, Eliot had expressed such an opinion after visiting Cuba—"a Paradise [where] the devil reigns"— as a young man. He wrote, "The lower classes—negro and Chinese and various half breeds—are more nearly brutes than anything I have ever known." Later, he managed to form a more benevolent opinion of the blacks he met while staying with a friend in Florida who owned an orange grove:

> As to the darkies I can't get enough of them. Our men are above average for they can read and write;

but such happy-go-lucky, merry, shiftless rascals as they all are! I never get tired of listening to them. I've seen a good deal of them for they work best with a white man bossing them all the while, and I have had that duty several times.[34]

Eliot's attitude was clearly paternalistic. He viewed blacks, not as peers, but rather as fascinating children who unquestionably needed supervision. On the same trip he had the opportunity to teach at Hampton Institute, and in his later years he was a board member at Hampton and other major black schools in the South.

Eliot's apparent efforts to overcome his own ignorance were consistently undermined by his prejudices. In 1933 he preached a sermon entitled "The Blight of Prejudice" and in it he said, "Race prejudice has not a single scientific leg to stand on. Negro inferiority has no scientific justification." Here his attitude seems to have matured, but in the next sentence he refers to Booker T. Washington and asserts "that thrift, skills, intelligence and character are the fundamental things for the race to secure."[35] Surely blacks needed education and skills, but to say they needed intelligence and character contradicts his previous statement. The conflict in Eliot's own mind over the abilities of blacks to carry out their own programs consistently led him to believe that blacks were not ready for what Brown was attempting to do.

"The blight of prejudice" of which Eliot spoke is ironically most apparent in the attitude Cornish showed toward Ethelred Brown. It peppers his correspondence with people who wrote inquiring about Brown's work. To one William S. Jones he wrote, "Mr. Brown is a negro and has the facility of speech and lack of foresight which sometimes go with the negro temperament."[36] Elsewhere he advises:

> I am told that [Brown] shows the emotional tempera-
> ment of his race and perhaps a weakness in judgment
> . . . I have lived much among negroes and am inclined to
> be very sympathetic with their temperamental pecu-
> liarities. They are very loveable people and often very
> child-like. It would be at once unjust and misleading
> to judge Mr. Brown as you would an Anglo-Saxon.[37]

In a biography of her husband, Cornish's wife describes
an early experience that contributed to his attitude toward blacks:

> Because he was small and sickly [Cornish] was no
> match for the big, rough boys in the public school
> and had to use his wits to survive. Among the boys
> was one called "Commodore," a tall and strong Negro
> who was backward in his studies, and so was in class
> with much younger boys. With him Louis Cornish
> made a pact. He would drive Commodore to school
> so many times a week in the pony cart and in return
> Commodore would fight boys who attacked little
> Louis. The plan worked admirably, and the two be-
> came fast friends.[38]

Mrs. Cornish also recounts an event from her husband's
adult life that is emblematic of his attitude toward blacks:

> They were motoring from Boston to Cambridge at
> the crowded hour when a driver from behind ran into
> their car. Louis Cornish's annoyance flared, but on
> getting out and finding that the offender was a badly
> frightened Negro, his mood instantly changed to one

of compassion and he seemed anxious only to put the other at ease.[39]

Why the sudden change in attitude? Was it because he believed this man was backward like his friend Commodore, irresponsible like Brown, and temperamentally immature like all black people? It is apparent that Cornish did not recognize blacks as peers. In his mind, unconscious racial bias, cultural narrowness, and paternalism held sway. It is not surprising, therefore, that he treated Brown as he did throughout the years of their association.

Such racial attitudes were pervasive at this time and it was natural that church officials were infected by them. This prejudice appears in Bygrave's report in comments like "those of his race who are fortunate enough to approach absolute whiteness." The attitude is implicit in Bygrave's astonishment at the intelligence and knowledge of the Jamaicans who questioned him after his addresses. Why should he have been surprised unless he had expected little? The statement most indicative of the extent of his racial prejudice was his recommendation that the work in Jamaica be viewed more as a "genuine humanitarian effort" than as a mission. He appealed to those Unitarians who were "more interested in social uplift effort than they [were] in . . . religious work." He seemed to be less concerned with blacks becoming Unitarians than with their becoming civilized. The spirit of his plea was the same as that shown in the Society for Propagating the Gospel among the Indians and Others in North America and in the financial support the American Unitarian Association gave to schools like Hampton and Tuskegee. The underlying attitude was that blacks must be uplifted morally and intellectually so that they could participate in the great white culture.

What was Brown's response to the racial attitudes that prevailed among the Unitarian officials? He did not hesitate to reinforce the obvious condescension with which they treated black people, and indeed he used it to accomplish his ends. His cooperation followed a pattern familiar among blacks—a survival tactic. With some justification, Brown saw himself as a "suffering servant." He wrote of how he had been wronged and deceived by the association, how the association had committed itself for "a long period of years," how the officers were too businesslike in their objectives for growth, how the church was desperately needed, and how the Jamaican mission should be viewed as an "exceptional child." His plea fed the directors' sense of paternalism and their guilt for the conditions under which blacks lived. It evoked their sympathy and their altruism. It was easy to strike these chords in this privileged class of Bostonians who considered it their moral obligation—noblesse oblige—to help the downtrodden black race. Their reward was the righteous feeling of guilt-soothing philanthropy, but with this feeling they did not acquire a sense of conviction, commitment, or understanding. Rather, they were left feeling that they should help improve the condition of blacks without having faith in the worth and ability of the very people they were striving to help. They sought to bring Unitarianism to people whose maturity of mind they doubted—a tragic dilemma born of cultural arrogance and destined to lead to failure.

Perhaps it reflects favorably upon Eliot and Cornish that they stood by their convictions in regard to the financing of the Jamaican mission rather than giving in to the impotent and fickle feeling of guilt. Nevertheless, they failed in their initial attempt to cut off Brown's funding, and Brown returned to Jamaica with what he thought was a long-term commitment. His narrative of this period continues:

> We won at that meeting. I later appeared before the Directors of the AUA and there won again with the result that the grant was re-voted and I returned to Jamaica (Parenthetically I may say here that I believe that victory was in effect a loss. I do believe that the President of the AUA never forgave me for all I said and for the friends I won, and his policy from then on was one of opposition, which it is clear, the Secretary [Cornish] now President approved). Kingston in spite of my attempt to keep it a secret knew of the withdrawal of the AUA. After 16 months of work, I returned to face not only a Kingston more hostile in 1916 than it was in 1914 but a sneering cynical city. Many city churches noticed us with special sermons. Mr. Bygrave's prophecy was fulfilled. Unitarianism became a scoff and a byeword and I was overcome with shame and confusion.
>
> As to the Whitfield Mission Church the simple folk who once welcomed us as angels of light disappointingly turned their backs on us. Ultimately we decided to cease operations and in the terms of the deed to return the land with our half finished church on it to the donor. And today the church is an Episcopalian church.—And it may have been ours.[40]

Brown was not yet deterred and elsewhere describes subsequent efforts prior to the association's final withdrawal of support:

We, however, started in again and not only regained lost ground but moved forward. Our membership was not large (but is this so unusual for the Unitarian churches?) but we were making friends even among orthodox ministers—white and colored—some of whom even went the length of lecturing in our hall on such topics as "the Modern Bible," "Agnosticism" and "Evolution," the last named having been given by no less a dignitary than the Lord Bishop of Jamaica. And then in the hour of our satisfaction, without rhymes or reason, as a bolt from the blue, the American Unitarian Association once again, in November, 1917, with Dr. Eliot as President and Dr. Cornish as Secretary, finally withdrew its support.[41]

The shock Brown expresses here at the association's withdrawal of financial support from the Jamaican movement indicates a great difference in outlook. In the letters that Brown and his wife wrote to Boston pleading for a renewal of financial aid, it is apparent that they expected their mission "to be treated as an exceptional child" and "to be financed for a long series of years," and they expected "the Association, as every other missionary body here has done and is doing, [to] support them until they grew"; furthermore, they "never expected [promised] 100 members in 4 years or a subscription role of $500."[42] They also argued that in Jamaica three hundred to four hundred members were necessary to support a church, other churches gave support without expecting immediate results, the combination of ministry and work that Brown had to follow was unknown in Jamaica and therefore hurt his efforts, and the church group was small because the social consequences of being a Unitarian were serious. In one letter Brown repeats a comment made by a prominent Jamaican that summarizes his feelings about the association:

No missionary Association could have done any *less*, and dozens have done infinitely more.[43]

The whole issue of mission work was viewed quite differently at 25 Beacon Street. The American Unitarian Association had become increasingly selective in the use of its funds. Eliot, who spent a great deal of his time traveling in support of the association's extension efforts,

followed in the established practice of most of the large home missionary societies of the other denominations [by making] annual grants to churches which were unable to support themselves financially. It was not long before Eliot became disillusioned with this traditional "subsidy system."[44]

Eventually he declared, "I do not believe in subsidizing churches. That policy is pauperizing and demoralizing." The preceding statements indicate that Eliot had broken with the practices of the other mission societies—the same practices upon which Mr. Walker, who had started the group in Alexandria, and Brown had built their expectations. It is therefore not surprising that Brown should think the association too concerned with numbers and money, but his utter amazement at the church's withdrawal was a reflection of his insensitivity to the denominational mood and his unwillingness to face the precariousness of the Jamaican situation.

Eliot's general attitude became standard policy for home missions of the American Unitarian Association and

generally governed policy for foreign missions as well. In
fact, early in Eliot's administration the association had
sent a man "to Cuba to investigate the feasibility of work
there. He recommended against establishing Unitarian
churches." In 1913 the first Unitarian Missionary Conference was held. It was poorly attended, and Eliot explained
this as being "indicative of the prevailing opinion that
foreign missionaries are more or less of an impertinence as
well as a waste of effort and money."[45] In addition to this,
the denomination was financially hard pressed due to
World War I.

Given this pragmatic approach to mission work and the
racial attitudes that informed the association's decisions, it
becomes even more difficult to comprehend why its officers gave Brown any money or encouragement. Their
choice was that of expediency, and in considering the
whole course of events, it becomes increasingly clear that
they gave him very little support of any kind. They discouraged him from attending seminary. Then shortly after
his ministry had begun, Hilary Bygrave advised Brown that
it was ill conceived. Less than a year later they transferred
him to Kingston, which meant he had to start over again.
Eighteen months after that, the association cut off funds
for the Jamaican mission, and the congregation consequently lost the church they had been constructing. To get
his grant reinstated, Brown had to abandon his work for
two months to travel to Boston. Two years later, the association again withdrew its support. There was no duplicity
intended on the part of the association: Lacking a real
commitment to Brown's effort, they withdrew when the
situation continued to seem impractical. From their perspective they had given Brown an adequate chance and had

made significant expenditures in Jamaica, but any Jamaican watching this process of fits and starts would have felt little confidence in the sincerity of the Unitarian denomination. It was largely Brown's single-mindedness that sustained him when the association waivered and then balked in its support. Brown writes of his situation and of his final years in Jamaica. He first recalls giving up a position that he believed would eventually result in a salary that would free him of his financial dependence on the church:

> It should here be noted that I agreed to leave Montego Bay in 1914 where I was an accountant to a large firm . . . On a gentleman's agreement, that if the work in Kingston showed it would be permanently backed by the AUA I gave up a good position on this understanding and in 3½ years I was deserted and left in a large city disillusioned and discredited. For a little over two years I struggled on against great odds and then decided to come to this country.[46]

Written eleven years after Brown came to the United States, his narrative does not convey the anger, the disillusionment, the agony, and the disgrace that Brown and his family felt. It does not mention that when Brown had visited Boston earlier, he had offered to remain in the United States to work in the black community there. Nor does it tell how his plea-filled letters received as a reply a simple copy of the directors' resolution withdrawing his funding along with a short expression of condolence. To carry on his mission in Kingston, he found a position as a junior master in the Wollmer School at a salary of sixty pounds a year. He worked there and continued the mission until January 1920, when he decided he would have to move to the United States to remedy the financial difficulties that plagued him in Jamaica.

Brown's financial situation raises one last issue in the abortion of the Jamaican mission. In a letter written in August 1918, Brown's eldest daughter appealed to the association for financial aid: "My father owes now about $150 for our schooling and for rent. He will be sued for these [funds]."[47] Presumably he weathered that crisis when a month later he acquired the position at the Wollmer School. But in January 1920, Brown himself wrote:

> After two years of vain effort to get my feet back on the commercial ladder, and after frantic efforts to make ends meet, I am now practically a bankrupt, owing nearly 120 pounds, and am at this moment facing public disgrace and ruin.
>
> My salvation is to leave for New York as early as possible. My health, my reputation, my future usefulness all demand this.[48]

These two incidents and Brown's earlier experience at the treasury indicate that he was regularly going into debt by living beyond his means. Perhaps he saw himself as the "exceptional child" whose excesses were to be tolerated.

The life style Brown preferred could not be maintained realistically by what he was able to provide. The B & FUA, after seeing his fiscal irresponsibility, had withdrawn their support early, and the AUA often expressed concern about where the money was going. (Cornish once estimated that eight thousand dollars had been given Brown.) Yet, Brown only infrequently gave an accounting of his funds. Apparently he used the funds as his needs demanded. At one point while he was receiving an AUA subsidy, he was sending his own children to private school, and with them, in return for the help his brother had given him when he had had difficulties with the civil service, he sent his brother's daughter. In Jamaica there was no other schooling available for his children—something he stressed rigorously and valued highly—if he did not pay for it. Brown, who had middle-class sensibilities if not means, must have seen many people living in abject poverty, and must have felt he was being asked to bear burdens different from those borne by any other Unitarian minister. He felt his situation was unjust, that many American Unitarians were prosperous, and yet he who had forsaken much and suffered much for the Unitarian cause had to pay the price alone.

Brown's idealism—his expectation of a better world, of an education for his children, of an enlightened religion for blacks—and his inability to make his ideals a reality because of racial prejudice and social intransigence are truly tragic. He confronted the same dilemma time and again in his life. This man possessed a vision, and he never ceased following it. It was his vision and hope that took him to New York City and Harlem, the black Mecca.

HARLEM

In a two-story brick house off a short street on a drab, gray day in mid-December, I sat facing Ethelred Brown's eldest child. On the outskirts of Jamaica, New York, where the bus turns around and heads back again, I listened to Mrs. Dorice Leslie speak of her life. A life in which she had often closed her eyes hoping she would open them to find it had all been a dream. It hadn't been, and now her seventy-ninth birthday was only three days away. She is the last of the Brown children. Ethelred, too, had survived all his siblings, as well as his wife and most of his children. He had the tenacity to hold on after everyone else had let go. He held on to life and to his dream of building a temple of liberal religion in Harlem until the last.

Dorice sat retrieving memories of her father. She would pause, then her animated voice would run on for a while, stop, and she would let out a sigh. She was happy that someone had finally taken an interest in her father's life story, but many of the memories still pained her. She remembered that twenty-four years earlier he had been growing sicker for over a year, but still his arms were strong and his face did not show his age. His complexion had simply turned darker. Gone too was the slender youth. His 5'8" frame had become stocky. He had always been a dignified man who carried himself well, no matter how hard the times. He never looked raggedy; his suit was always pressed. A bespectacled, scholarly man, he was personable, but not charismatic. He had few close friends, for his time was occupied with reading and writing, attending meetings, organizing, and speaking. The time that remained he spent with his family. To most people he presented the public man; he did not often betray his private sorrow.

At the age of eighty-one he found himself in Mt. Sinai Hospital; when the doctor asked him to stay, he protested that he had a meeting to attend in Boston. The doctor prevailed. Dorice came often to see him, never knowing how long it would be. John Haynes Holmes also visited him. A man who had suffered much in life did not suffer much in death. On February 17, 1956, after four weeks in the hospital, Egbert Ethelred Brown died. Dorice remembered that a little while before he went into the hospital, he had written to someone, "I hope 1956 will be the destiny of the church." Sadly, it was to be the year of his destiny, and he, in a real sense, was the spirit of that church, without him it languished. He had come a long way since he had sailed from Jamaica in 1920, exactly thirty-six years earlier. He had hoped to build a Unitarian church in Harlem, but what he left was less tangible. He touched lives, promoted radical causes, exposed others to a broad spectrum of issues, affected the tenor of his time in some small ways, but left no temple of liberal religion in Harlem.

When he and Ella arrived in Harlem in March 1920, it was home for two hundred thousand blacks. The Great Migration of blacks, in which two million people had moved to the North to work in the defense industries, had peaked in 1915. In 1905 when the great influx of blacks into New York had begun, black realty companies had leased and bought buildings in Harlem to rent to blacks. Harlem's whites had fought to keep them out, but were overwhelmed and then fled. There had even been a Unitarian church in Harlem—the Unity Congregational Society—but it was probably unwilling or unable to adjust to a black Harlem. It moved and became the Westside Unitarian Church in 1921.[49]

Harlem was transformed, and the community Brown joined was the center of the black world:

In the history of New York the name Harlem has changed from Dutch to Irish to Jewish to Negro; but it was through this last change that it has gained its most widespread fame. Throughout coloured America, Harlem is the recognized Negro capital. Indeed, it is Mecca for the sightseer, the pleasure seeker, the curious, the adventurous, the enterprising, the ambitious, and the talented of the entire Negro world; for the lure of it has reached down to every island of the Carib Sea and penetrated even into Africa. It is almost as well known in the white world, for it has been much talked and written about.[50]

Brown arrived in Harlem during "an extraordinary era—the fabulous twenties." This was a period of exceptional creativity known as the Harlem Renaissance in which "Negro artists poured out a stream of poems, plays and musical compositions."[51] Moreover, there were all kinds of institutional fervor, from the National Association for the Advancement of Colored People, to Marcus Garvey's United Negro Improvement Association, to the Communist party. Into the midst of this surging community, two men walked seeking their destinies: one was Brown, the other was Paul Robeson.

It is an interesting coincidence that Ethelred Brown arrived in New York City a month after Paul Robeson. Robeson, a young man who had just graduated from Rutgers, was already famous as an all-American football player; he had come to study law at Columbia University. Robeson lived in Harlem, and he quickly became a vital part of the Harlem Renaissance.

When Ethelred Brown came to the black Mecca, he was forty-five years old. The previous eight years he had struggled unsuccessfully to establish Unitarianism in Jamaica. He came to Harlem to start anew.

Paul Robeson would quickly leave the law profession to become the foremost black entertainer in America. He would be acclaimed throughout the world, but would subsequently become infamous in his homeland for using his art to make radical political statements. He would become an eloquent spokesman for all oppressed peoples. Like Brown, he would make a midlife change of direction, and dedicate himself to a cause that would bring him long years of persecution and suffering.

Brown's suffering had already begun in Jamaica. He had decided on the ministry as his calling, and he was determined to pursue it for the rest of his life; but unlike Robeson, whose success was astronomical and whose fall was deep, Brown's path would be a slow climb out of obscurity.

In a terrible storm on a bitterly cold afternoon my wife and I landed in New York on February 27, 1920, leaving our six children with their grandparents in Montego Bay. The voyage of faith was to begin.

I believed in and still believe in Unitarianism as the religion of the future—the religion with an emancipating message which all peoples of every race may understand and accept—I had then and still have faith in this race of mine and found very soon then in Harlem there were not so many Negroes as plain human beings—conservatives, liberals and radicals—men and women who had long since outgrown intellectually and morally the fundamental teachings of the older churches—and without conceit I had and still have faith in myself—faith in my patience in my courage—faith in my faith—not things to boast of but graces to be deeply thankful for.

Without much delay I set out to carry out the purpose of my trip to Harlem, namely, to establish a Unitarian church, and on Sunday evening, March 7, 1920, seven of us met in the Lafayette Hall, the cradle of many a Harlem church, and then and there organized a church named in honor of John Haynes Holmes, the only ministerial friend of those early days, the Harlem Community Church.[52]

For many years Holmes and Brown hoped to create some sort of affiliate status for the Harlem church; this never came to pass, but Brown's association with Holmes was a lasting one. Holmes proved to be one of Brown's main supporters in his continuing battle with the American Unitarian Association. On his arrival, Brown's relationship with the church officials was strained, and he understandably took up his new mission without seeking any financial support from the denomination.

Like Paul of Tarsus, Brown had to work at his trade while he preached the gospel. In Jamaica, Brown's ability to find suitable employment outside the church enabled him to carry on his religious work, but in New York this was not the case. It was not uncommon to find black college graduates working in the post office; underemployment was the rule, not the exception. Even Paul Robeson found that he could not practice law because the American Bar Association discriminated against blacks. Later he quit a position as a law clerk when a secretary refused to type for him. Similarly, Brown found he was unable to locate a position as an accountant, the work that had been his mainstay in Jamaica. In his "Brief History of the Harlem Unitarian Church," Brown lists his succession of jobs and the recurring financial hardships he faced during his first twenty years in New York:

> I worked as an elevator operator at a downtown hotel for 5½ years, being at the church only on alternate Sunday evenings. Following this I was a speaker for the Socialist Party for three years. Then followed a period of real hardship, and then there came a break in my favor when in 1929 I secured the position of

Office Secretary of "The World Tomorrow," in which position I continued to work until the magazine ceased publication in July 1934. Then followed another period of hard times. The Rev. Dale DeWitt, Regional Director of the American Unitarian Association . . . discovered me in 1937 as a recipient of public relief. He set out at once to seek relief from this unsatisfactory condition, and succeeded in securing an appropriation from the AUA of $50.00 a month which I received from November 1937 to July 1939—a period of 21 months. When I reached my 65th birthday on July 11, 1940, I became eligible for a pension which I received, and am still receiving. The above is the financial story of the minister of the Harlem Unitarian Church from March 1920 to July 1940—a period of 20 years.[53]

Brown's struggles to maintain his family in a racist society were trying enough, but unknown to him the American Unitarian Association was hampering his church work as well. In October 1921, a year and a half after Brown arrived in Harlem, Louis Cornish wrote the following letter to a Mr. McDougall, who had requested information about Brown:

I speak I believe with no anti-negro feeling . . . It is only fair to say that there are those who [in reference to Jamaica] claim Mr. Brown was frankly dishonest. I prefer another interpretation. I do not think he ever used any money with conscious dishonesty, but as his need was pressing—I think he has nine children and his salary was small—with true negro reckoning there was always a bright tomorrow when he could pay the debts of today . . . There are those who believe that he deliberately tried to deceive, but I believe the negro

has an extraordinary histrionic vein, and what a man
expects to accomplish and what he is actually doing
blend happily into reality.

He wrote me a few weeks ago asking for hymn
books for his Community Church at Harlem, which
I am afraid you will find exists only on paper. He
preaches there once a fortnight, and I suspect that
the congregation as in Jamaica is made up largely of
his household.

. . . I frankly counsel that you give him no encouragement whatever in the way of financial assistance
or promise of help to his church.[54]

This letter did not stop Mr. McDougall from speaking at
the Harlem Community Church, but Brown reported that
his address, calling for a closer affiliation with the parent
association, was not well received.

Cornish may have been correct in his suspicion about
Brown's use of the funds, but I am reluctant to accept a
judgment so riddled with racial prejudice. He dismissed
Brown's personal idiosyncrasies as racial afflictions. He
claimed Brown had nine children and later said thirteen
when there were only six. Finally, the church, which he
speculated comprised only Brown's household, actually
had an average membership of thirty during its first three
years and an income of $730, of which Brown only received
$68.56. This was the attitude of the man with whom Brown
would have to deal over the next sixteen years, first as the
administrative vice-president and then as the president of
the American Unitarian Association. It is no wonder that
Brown should rage at "the remarkably strange antagonism
of the AUA to religious work among Negroes."

In 1925 Brown found himself maneuvered into a Catch-
22 situation. George F. Patterson, the secretary of the

fellowship committee, wrote to ask why the committee should not strike Brown's name from the ministerial rolls. The committee argued that since he was employed in a position other than as a minister, and since his church was "not in sympathy with the Unitarian spirit and purpose,"[55] they should remove his name unless he proved otherwise. Outraged, Brown replied, first, that he could not engage in a full-time ministry because the church did not have the wherewithal to pay him and the denomination would give him no support. He was forced to work full time in other capacities in order to support his family and could only minister in his remaining time. The second charge was simply false; he was and had always been a Unitarian minister.[56] After they heard from Brown, the committee took no action.

Brown always insisted that his position as an "elevator boy," which he rightfully felt was beneath his dignity, projected a poor image and indicated such an indifference toward him on the part of the denomination that he was seriously hindered in his efforts to form a viable church. He persevered in his mission, and was fortuitously discovered by the Socialist party late in 1925, when he became one of their speakers. He was brought to the attention of the Socialists by some of the members of his church who were among the small group of left-wing radicals in Harlem. After finding this job, Brown had more time for his church and could preach every Sunday. But this arrangement did not end his problems. Although in one place he wrote that he worked for the Socialists for three years, in a letter written in November 1926 he reported "my engagement with the Socialist Party is at an end." Presumably this was because the campaign was over; apparently, he

worked for them preceding elections for three years. In the
same letter he continues, "I hesitate to return to the former
unsatisfactory arrangement."[57] The problem he faced was
how to continue his church work without returning to a
job as a menial laborer that not only hampered him but
was odious as well.

Earlier in 1926 Brown had written Samuel A. Eliot asking for support of the fledgling church in Harlem. Eliot
referred the matter to the Reverend Walter R. Hunt, the
association's field secretary in New York, and also suggested that Brown appeal to his friends and neighbors in
New York. In response to a second letter, Eliot tersely repeated that the matter was in Hunt's hands and that he
would not acknowledge further communication from
Brown. Brown then sent several letters to Hunt. The first
appealed for aid so that he might devote himself full time
to the Harlem Community Church, which now claimed a
membership of eighty-five and expenditures totaling
$1,128.30. In a second letter sent two days later, Brown,
in a confessional manner, reviewed the history of his relationship with the American Unitarian Association, hoping
that once Hunt understood his plight, Hunt would assist
him: "So much of the past, the present and the future is
wrapped up in this work and so much of this work's future
is in my own hands I have decided to give you a view of the
personal." Brown then recounted his trials and suffering in
Jamaica. Finally he added:

Something I have never mentioned even to my friend
John Haynes Holmes, my poor wife has never recov-
ered from the disappointment. [She couldn't understand and] today her mind is deranged and her

talking—rambling, incoherent—is of the church that ruined us.[58]

These letters brought no support from the American Unitarian Association.

Faced with official indifference, the end of his engagement with the Socialist party, and Ella's mental deterioration, Brown decided in 1926 to write directly to other ministers in the denomination. He specifically requested their financial assistance. Many ministers responded to this solicitation by saying they thought it was the association's province to support his efforts. Others sent small donations, and one wrote, "The AUA finds money to support our work among Finns, Icelanders, Italians and other foreign populations and yet it seems they can find no funds to foster a work among Afro-Americans."[59]

Brown's appeal failed to raise the necessary funds, but it became the issue around which the fellowship committee, for the second time, considered dropping his name in February 1928. Patterson, the secretary of the fellowship committee, revealed his attitude toward Brown in a letter to another Unitarian minister: "He is continually soliciting our churches . . . he actually lives by begging for a cause that is generally recognized as beginning and ending in himself and his family."[60]

This time the removal of Brown's name was only prevented by the intervention of John Haynes Holmes. Holmes wrote a letter challenging the committee's right to remove Brown's name, asking if they were taking this action because of his race. Holmes then listed a large number of men whom he knew to be no longer involved in the Unitarian ministry and yet their names remained in the yearbook. The committee ignored Holmes's arguments, overlooked the absence of specific guidelines that prohibited solicitation, and agreed to keep Brown's name on the list of ministers only because Holmes guaranteed that Brown would not solicit Unitarian churches.

Stymied by the Unitarian officials in his attempt to get financial aid and attacked by the fellowship committee, Brown wrote directly to the directors of the association, listing his grievances. Among these were the association officials' unresponsiveness to the needs of the Harlem church, the fellowship committee's two attempts to remove his name from the ministerial rolls, and the embarrassing response of the Committee on Ministerial Aid to one of his personal appeals. This last appeal for money arose as the result of a court case in which Brown was found to be in arrears in his rent payments. He had appealed to the association for financial assistance and then found that, unbidden by and unannounced to him, they had referred his name to a public charity in New York City—a situation he found particularly embarrassing and highly unethical. He called the act a "deliberate attempt to humiliate me." The church officials' intent had been to render Brown assistance without seeming to lend denominational support to his cause or to appear to accept responsibility for his well-being. But Brown interpreted their act as an effort "to punish the man in charge because he is stubbornly carrying on the work instead of quitting as they desire."[61] Brown concluded his letter by saying he was certain these things were done without the directors' knowledge and that they would do their best to rectify the situation.

Dealing with the American Unitarian Association was only one problem among many for Brown. He was also hard pressed by a home situation that often reached a crisis level, and it is hard to exaggerate the anguish Ethelred often felt. His second son, who was an alcoholic and was eventually committed to an asylum, had once taken Brown's one good suit—his preaching suit—and pawned it. His wife, Ella, had been unable to cope with the poverty, the trials, and the disappointments. She had played the piano at the church for a time, but when she began making mistakes, some of the members insisted she not continue. Ella did little at home and spent her time wandering around the streets. At times she went to Holmes' Community Church of New York where John Haynes Holmes ministered dressed improperly, and at other times she fell asleep there. Finally, Holmes had to tell Brown to try and keep her from coming to the church. The duty of nursing his wife and tending to the household chores fell to Brown even though his daughters helped him as much as they could.

In the fall of 1928 Brown resumed writing letters of solicitation to his Unitarian colleagues. Holmes sent this response to an inquiry about the letters from Patterson:

> This letter which you sent me signed by Mr. Brown is similar to the one which has come to me . . . In answer to your inquiry I can say that I heartily disapprove of Mr. Brown's writing to his fellow ministers in this fashion, that I have warned him against it, and that he has agreed not to do it. I am sorry that he has resorted to this practice again.
>
> On the other hand, and most emphatically, I want to say that Mr. Brown is in a real distressing condition of misery. His plight is sad beyond words. He has no employment, his wife is feeble-minded and a dreadful case, his oldest son is out of employment, and his second son is in the insane asylum. The man needs help

in the worst way and if any of the brethren want
to help him out, the money will not be wasted. I
am sending Mr. Brown a Christmas donation from
this church.[62]

Now Brown's situation went from bad to worse. In
March 1929 Brown's eldest son, Howard, committed suicide.
Dorice, Brown's daughter, recalled the events of that day:

Howie was living at home then. I was at home then
too. Oh! Father felt so guilty because he didn't know
he was so sick. Howie was working all the time but he
had gotten quiet and didn't want to go about looking
for a job. That morning father must have said, "Why
are you sitting here like a bum? Why don't you go
out and find a job?" Later father went out to get a
paper and when he came back . . . Can you imagine
how he felt because he was the last person who spoke
to him? To come back up and go into the bathroom.
I don't know how he didn't faint. It's not an easy
thing to see and father had to witness it alone. No-
body was there. He had to take him down by himself.
He was alone. He cried and cried and cried.[63]

Prior to Howard's suicide, the members of the Harlem
church had drafted a general appeal for money to help
Brown, who they knew was in grave financial difficulty.
Now they hurriedly added a note about the death of
Brown's son, wrote "urgent" across the top, and sent it.
The appeal received a generous response from Holmes
and a few others, but it also provoked a particularly scath-
ing letter about Brown from the Unitarian headquarters
in New York to Walter Hunt in Boston:

Here is another one! It seems as though something ought to be done to make this man understand that until he gets out and does some real work to support his family he has no chance of any help. No wonder his son committed suicide, he must have been the only wise one in the family.

Everyone around here reports a very good Easter congregation and much interest as a result of the advertising material.[64]

The writer's insensitivity blinded him to the irony of his own letter. His callous reference to the death of Brown's son is all the more shocking in a letter discussing Easter events. Remarkably, the writer felt no contradiction in attacking Brown's solicitations while lauding the positive results of his own advertising.

This letter is representative of the prevailing hostile sentiments expressed about Brown within the American Unitarian Association. Shortly after his son's death Brown discovered that a special committee had been established by the directors to review his situation. He quickly wrote the Reverend Frank Wicks protesting that he had not been informed. In addition, Brown requested assistance from the Ministerial Aid Fund, but he did not receive even a word of sympathy in return. Brown had earlier written to tell Cornish, now the president, of his son's death, and he mentioned in his letter to Wicks the failure of another colleague to respond:

I lied to my wife a moment ago. Poor soul! She asked me if Dr. Cornish had not sent a word of sympathy. I told her he had. But (would you believe it?) he has not.

... No wonder my poor boy became an Atheist
and then gave up the fight.[65]

The failure of both Cornish and Wicks to respond at this
time is another example of the association's attitude.
Brown had come to be viewed as a nuisance, not simply by
a few association officials but by the board of directors as
well. Brown himself had heard thirdhand through the psy-
chiatrist attending his wife that he "had" made the directors "so mad by [his] insistence in throwing the responsibility for [his] work up to them that although they now
knew that they [had] done wrong they dare not go back on
themselves."[66] Not unsurprisingly, on May 23, 1929, after
studying the situation, the directors told the fellowship
committee to drop Brown's name. This action provoked
a series of angry appeals from Brown, charging them
with racism.

It was not until two years later that another committee
was established to look into the circumstances surround-
ing the removal of Ethelred Brown's name from the ministerial rolls, and for the first time Brown was given a chance
to present his side of the story. The committee in its report
of April 1932 found all parties at fault. The committee
came to six main conclusions:

1. There were no rules of the Fellowship Committee
   under which Mr. Brown could have been dismissed . . .
2. The Committee finds conclusively . . . that the
   Fellowship Committee . . . dropped him . . . because he was a nuisance to the denomination . . .

3. The Committee finds that Mr. Brown . . . agreed unequivocally to cease his solicitation . . .
4. The Committee finds . . . from the admission of Mr. Brown at the hearing that Mr. Brown did not keep this promise . . . and that although there were mitigating circumstances in some instances, the objectionable solicitation continued.
5. The Committee finds that Mr. Brown is wholly sincere in his work and is making a very real endeavor to found a liberal church for the negroes in New York, but the Committee is forced to the conclusion that Mr. Brown is nevertheless entirely irresponsible.
6. The Committee finds that the Fellowship Committee was unwise in that it did not give Mr. Brown a hearing and that it did not follow its own rules in dealing with Mr. Brown's case, but the Committee further finds that the Fellowship Committee was supported in every instance by the Board of Directors and the Board of Directors were equally at fault.[67]

In the end the committee was split in its recommendation as to whether or not to readmit Brown into fellowship. The board sustained its earlier decision. Brown, who never saw the full report, received no explanation whatsoever, only a short note announcing the decision. Again, Brown fired off a number of angry letters. Finally, in 1934 Brown enlisted the help of the American Civil Liberties Union to win back his fellowship. Faced with this challenge by "a Jewish lawyer of the type we might expect to be active in the affairs of the" ACLU, as one Unitarian official commented, the fellowship committee grudgingly readmitted

Brown on May 8, 1935.[68] The readmittance was contingent upon Brown's commitment not to solicit Unitarian ministers or churches.

Times had changed. Louis Cornish's presidency would end in 1937, and already new men held sway at 25 Beacon Street. In January 1937 Charles Joy, administrative vice-president of the association, spoke at the Harlem Unitarian Church to a group of eighty. He found there were forty-five active members and he recommended that the church's application for membership in the American Unitarian Association be accepted. He wrote, "I was much impressed with the quality of the group."[69] But when he returned to Boston and tried to get an appropriation for the church, to his surprise "Louis [Cornish] would not consent. He seems to feel very bitter about it all, and so blocked it. Louis even questioned the accuracy of Brown's statement that he was getting relief."[70]

Brown was receiving public relief, but this had not been the case between 1929 and 1934, when he worked as the office manager for the *World Tomorrow*, a magazine that represented the views of socialist and pacifist religionists and liberals. Among its editors were Reinhold Niebuhr and Paul H. Douglas, and among its contributing editors were John Haynes Holmes, H. Richard Niebuhr, Norman Thomas, and A. J. Muste. Brown worked with the *World Tomorrow* until publication ceased in 1934.[71] Then, at the age of fifty-eight and in the middle of the Great Depression, he was without a job. He got by for a while on the recently received share of his father's estate and on the money the editors of the *World Tomorrow* had collected for him. But those were hard times, as one writer reminds us:

> During the Great Depression, North America, in the words of Lester Granger, "almost fell apart." There was a bitter bit of poetry: the Negro, Last Hired and First Fired. Business tightened their belts and bade their Negro employees good-bye. Matrons cut their budgets and domestics went home and looked at empty larders. By 1935 about one out of every 4 negroes in America was on relief. The need in urban areas was appalling.[72]

Brown was among those on relief. He was jobless, as were his two youngest children, who had reached employment age during the depression.

Brown's life involved far more than the personal crises and recurring battles with the Unitarian officials I have focused on. To capture all the dimensions of his character, one must look beyond his home life and beyond the confines of the denomination. Two other important elements must be woven into the fabric of his life story—his political involvements and his guidance of the religious life of the Harlem Unitarian Church. As we continue to examine his life, I will weave these two strands into his story, because they contain the essence of the message Brown brought to Harlem and that community's response.

Throughout crises and hard times Brown's work with the church never ceased. The church was small and raising money was never an easy matter. In Brown's words, "Negroes, however intelligent and cultured, are poor, because in America they are elevator men and porters."[73] Brown would explain this to affluent white Unitarians, but they never really understood him. Brown's church was like many other black churches—poor. "Studies have shown that while there were large, community-conscious congregations most black churches were small, ineffectual and the problem of paying the minister's salary kept these congregations struggling for survival."[74] It is a tribute to Brown that the Harlem church lasted as long as it did. Had his salary been foremost in his mind, the church would not have existed at all. During its existence, Brown's church had three different names. Initially it was known as the Harlem Community Church. In 1928 it changed its name to the Hubert Harrison Memorial Church after a popular Harlem educator, and finally, in 1937, after becoming formally affiliated with the AUA, to the Harlem Unitarian Church.

One of these "large, community-conscious congregations" was the Abyssinian Baptist Church, where the Adam Clayton Powells, Senior and Junior, ministered. It was one of the few liberal orthodox churches in Harlem, and with fifteen thousand members it was also one of the largest. The Powells were active in social reform, and the younger Powell, a graduate of Union Theological Seminary, was a theological liberal. Brown was known and respected in Harlem and in the Powells' religious community as both a political radical and a religious liberal, and during the late 1930s was frequently invited to preach at their church.

From his youth onward Brown had a strong sense of justice. Dorice had heard that, as a child, Ethelred had been disturbed by the presence of maids at home and he had told his parents not to be so harsh with them. This was a concern he pursued all his life. While still in Jamaica, he was "actively involved in organizing the Negro Progressive

Association and the Liberal Association." The general aims of both were to foster race pride, to promote economic progress, and to secure rights for all blacks. Brown was well known for his interests in this area: "During the labor disturbances that swept Jamaica in 1918–19, Rev. Brown emerged as a militant spokesman of the cause of the workers. He also wrote an essay, 'Labor Conditions in Jamaica Prior to 1917,' which was published in the *Journal of Negro History* in October 1919."[75] In Harlem, this concern for others continued. He would fire off a letter after reading an article that described an incident of segregation, discrimination, or police brutality. On one occasion he wrote a letter of protest to the police department. Dorice recalled that "they sent an inspector down because they were ready for trouble. Father was ready. But when the officer saw the place, the humble apartment in which the man sat who had written *such* a letter, he was shocked."[76]

Brown considered civic involvement central to his ministry. He was a member of the Harlem Job Committee and the Harlem Tenants League. The former group reached an agreement with the Uptown Chamber of Commerce by which its members promised to hire blacks for one third of its white-collar jobs. Typically, one of the founding members of the Harlem church, Frank Crosswaith, who was the head of the Harlem Job Committee, denounced the plan. Such disagreements were not uncommon among members of the Harlem church. Brown had other causes. For example, he thought it was important to promote cooperative rather than profit-making enterprises. In an article in the *Amsterdam News*, Harlem's major newspaper, he challenged Harlem's leading churches to start a cooperative store, an enterprise he had earlier promoted in Jamaica.

Shaking black churches out of their complacency was another one of Brown's concerns. In a letter to the editor of the same paper, Brown wrote:

> The Negro . . . has too much of the wrong kind of religion . . . The kind which encourages him to transfer his interest from here and now to some existence in some otherworld, [which embraces] servile contentment instead of provoking rebellious discontentment . . . which destroys his personal responsibility by leading him to believe in the possibility of escaping punishment for his wrong doing.
>
> [What is needed is] a religion of the present and the practical profoundly concerned with this world . . . The virtue of discontentment is a necessary preliminary to making this earth a place wherein dwell justice and peace and love . . . [Every man must] shoulder his own responsibility [and] every man must work out his own salvation.
>
> Our colored ministers must . . . cleanse their religious meetings from the over-emotionalism which dangerously borders on fanaticism.[77]

Brown protested against churches that focused on otherworldly concerns rather than on bringing justice into this world. People knew him and his ideas, and his letters and statements frequently appeared in the Harlem newspapers and stimulated much discussion.

Brown was also concerned about his homeland, Jamaica. He was chairman of the Jamaican Benevolent Association, vice-president of the Federation of Jamaican Organizations, and one of the founders and president of the Jamaican Progressive League. In one of these capacities he would, on occasion, help people in difficulty with the immigration office of the port of New York. He spoke from experience when he appeared as a witness before President Truman's Commission on Immigration, and was forthright in his request to be heard: "Advised that no representative of West Indian organizations intended to appear, he presented in person a written request to be heard and was at the last moment of the hearing permitted to testify."[78] His greatest honor came in 1938 when he was sent to Jamaica to represent the Progressive League before the West Indies royal commission studying Jamaican independence. When he arrived one old friend said jokingly, "Oh, Egbert! Don't come back here starting trouble."[79] They knew what kind of man he was, and many respected him for standing up to white authority. Further recognition came because of his dedication to the welfare of his native land, a dedication that equaled his loyalty to liberal religion. After Jamaica became independent, Brown was the one individual chiefly responsible for raising funds in the United States to help finance the election campaigns of the People's National party.[80] In 1952 Mr. Norman Manely, then prime minister of Jamaica, invited him to return home as a guest of the party.

Brown's concerns embraced more than abstract causes. He befriended a prison inmate, carried on a long correspondence with him, and on at least one occasion visited him. Dorice remembered that once at Christmas time she walked into the bedroom and found her father hiding a present for the prisoner. Brown had so little that giving to this man was like taking away from himself, and Brown knew Dorice would not be happy about that.

As Brown struggled to serve the many ideas and individuals he was concerned with, some Unitarian ministers slowly came to realize that Brown was a significant figure in Harlem. In 1939 John H. Lathrop, minister of the First Unitarian Congregationalist Society of Brooklyn, wrote to A. Powell Davies, the chairman of the Department of Unitarian Extension and Church Maintenance:

> But the potency of our movement is not in the numbers and finance of our gathering there. Mr. Brown carries the Unitarian flag with wide reaching influence throughout the community. He would be easily worth supporting if he had no Sunday night of his own . . . He brings his influence to bear in all sorts of ways under the Unitarian banner, as he does, for example, in some of the negro newspapers.[81]

When Lathrop wrote this in 1939, Brown's fortunes within the denomination had already changed.

Beginning in 1937, with the advent of Frederick May Eliot's administration, prospects had improved for Ethelred Brown. Through the support of Dale DeWitt, the association's field representative in New York, Brown began to receive the financial and moral backing he had sought for so many years. It was then for the first time that the Harlem Unitarian Church came under the watchful eye of the Department of Unitarian Extension and Church maintenance. Brown made quarterly reports to this committee, which gave him guidance and financial aid. This support ended suddenly when World War II began and the association found itself strapped financially, but this time the loss of support was more financial than moral and did not last long. A year later, Brown turned sixty-five and became eligible for the minister's service pension, which helped sustain him until the end of his life. His sixty-fifth birthday fell in the same year as the church's twentieth anniversary, and both occasions were marked together by a celebration at which the denomination was well represented.

The new favorable attitude of the American Unitarian Association toward Brown was due in part to the different racial attitude of the new generation. It was also indicative of a change in political sentiments. In his "Brief History of the Harlem Unitarian Church," Brown asks this question: "What relationship if any did the fact that the foundation members of the church were socialists bear to the early trials of the movement?" The answer has far-reaching implications, and while he left it unanswered, I cannot. Richard B. Moore, Grace Campbell, W. A. Domingo, and Frank Crosswaith, who in 1920 were charter members of the church, were also among "the most prominent of the very few Negro Socialists, or sympathizers of the time."[82] They were involved in the split between the Socialist and the Communist parties. Moore and Campbell went with the Communists, and Domingo and Crosswaith went with the Socialists. Brown was aligned with the Socialists, and besides being one of their speakers, he ran for the Assembly on the Socialist ticket. The strategies of the two parties were different. The Socialists sought a legal, nonviolent transformation of society, the Communists looked forward to a social revolution, and both groups made basic errors in their efforts in Harlem. The Socialist Eugene Debs, unable to grasp the uniqueness of the black situation or the racist mentality of America, said, "We have nothing special to offer the Negro."[83] The Communists, on the other hand, energetically wooed blacks, but "failed to understand that Negroes, perhaps more than whites, were fundamentally American in the sense that they aspired to equality of

opportunity, or at least, to getting ahead within the existing institutional structure rather than through any radical
reorganization of society."[84] Indeed, the theoretical and
tactical differences with which these few black political
activists were absorbed held little meaning for the destitute
blacks in Harlem.

Yet "in subsequent years this split among the Negro
Socialists was the root cause of more destructive rivalry in
Harlem civil rights and labor politics than the record reveals."[85] This was evident in what happened to the Harlem
church. Brown recalled that there "occurred what may be
rightly called a communist invasion, and with this began
our troubles. The standard of our meetings deteriorated;
the discussions fell from the high level attained and became
irrelevant, abusive and vulgar."[86] Brown circumvented the
situation by shifting from the typical forum service to a
more distinctly religious service.

The identification of Brown and some of the founding
members of the church with radical political stances obviously influenced the church's appeal within Harlem,
especially since the black community was essentially conservative. It also made the church suspect to some of the
earlier denomination officials. George Patterson once wrote
to Lathrop, who inquired about Brown, "[One] person
attended his meeting and reported it as a Bolshevist gathering."[87] Meanwhile several Unitarian ministers who were
fellow Socialists, after receiving Brown's appeals for money
in which he announced that he was at present a speaker for
the Socialist party, cautioned him that such statements
could be counterproductive. One wrote:

Most of our ministers are rather conservative and
what you call the distasteful and incongruous work

of an elevator operator appeals far more to them as honorable than addressing crowds for the Socialist Party.[88]

The situation of the Harlem Unitarian Church was further complicated by the tensions between the West Indian and black American communities. This issue does not often emerge in Brown's own writings, but when it did he reveals a deep concern that these two communities overcome the prejudice and antagonism they harbored toward one another.[89] Harold Cruse in *The Crisis of the Negro Intellectual* reports a number of reasons for the problems between these two communities. Primarily, "the islanders presented a threat of competition for the jobs available to blacks."[90] There was also a tendency for the Afro-Caribbeans to deal with discrimination by emphasizing that they were not Afro-Americans but rather British subjects. The tensions between these groups were pervasive, and they affected the church in subtle and intangible ways. Dorice Leslie did not recall any problems in this regard, but Benjamin Richardson, a black Harvard Divinity student who preached at the Harlem church, reported "a schism between the American Negroes and the West Indian Negroes."[91] G. Peter Fleck, a member of the New York extension committee who visited the church during Brown's later years, found the congregation to be largely Jamaican.[92] It seems that was an issue. In reading Brown's sermons one does not find references to black American writers but rather, occasionally, to Claude McKay, the West Indian poet, and still more frequently to Ralph Waldo Emerson and Alfred Lord Tennyson. This is particularly strange, since Brown lived at the high point of the Harlem Renaissance; it leads one to believe that he did not appreciate the black American psyche.

Brown was involved in several other struggles as well. Several of his church members, such as Hodge Kirnon and W. A. Domingo, were supporters of Marcus Garvey; Brown may even have worked for Garvey's United Negro Improvement Association when he first arrived in Harlem. But at some point, Domingo, Richard B. Moore, Frank Crosswaith, and Thomas Potter, all members of the Harlem church, became Garvey's "bitterest and most persistent opponents."[93] Brown shared their sentiments. In fact, it appears that a rivalry between Brown and Garvey existed even during their early years in Jamaica. In a letter to a follower in Jamaica dated May 12, 1916, Garvey wrote, "I noticed in the papers that the 'Jamaica League' crowd who have been trying to upset the association are trying to form an association through E. E. Brown to befool the negro and make selfish capital out of him. I will handle them when I return to Jamaica."[94] This longstanding antagonism led to a catastrophic Sunday evening service in January 1928. It made the headlines of the *Amsterdam News:* "Harlem Preacher Hit on Head at Sunday Service." The article read:

> The Rev. Mr. Brown began his address about 8:30 and told his audience that Marcus Garvey was a good Propagandist, a crowd collector and a money getter, but a bad leader. "While I do not approve of deportation as such, I heartily approve of Marcus Garvey's deportation, which was better for America in general and the Negro in particular," said the Rev. Brown.
>
> At this junction a native African Garveyite rose to defend his leader. The Rev. Brown allowed him 20 minutes in which to speak. He defended Garvey with such eloquence that he threw the church in an uproar, mostly against the pastor.

The minister then announced that he would allow anyone in the audience who purported to speak for Garvey of the U.N.I.A. 10 minutes, or would prolong the speaker's time 10 minutes. A woman in the audience demanded that the speaker's time be prolonged indefinitely, which the Rev. Mr. Brown would not grant. Thereupon a number of alleged Garvey adherents stalked out of the church uttering unkind expletives.

"Now that the rowdies are leaving," said the pastor, "we may continue with the discussion." Rowdies? The crowd became infuriated and one man turned to strike down the reverend but someone restrained him. "I will not tolerate this disorder!" thundered the Rev. Mr. Brown. "The meeting is closed!"

The minister picked up his prayer book and retired to another room, which was unlighted. As he stepped inside he felt a staggering blow on the head and turned and saw a man fleeing. He turned on the light and saw himself covered with blood. The police were called, but no arrest was made. The assailant had escaped.[95]

One finds it hard to imagine this wild scene or the "communist invasion" occurring within the context of a worship service. But that they happened is instructive, for they reveal that there was a strong political element—an element found to be common in both Unitarianism and black religion—incorporated into the religious life of the Harlem Unitarian Church. Political freedom emerged as a central element in Brown's ministry and as a significant aspect of the lives of a number of church members. While Brown railed at the black churches in Harlem for pursuing otherworldly concerns, he endeavored to make the connection between religion and politics intimate. This is often not a harmonious union, and it points to a central uncertainty in the life of the church. Brown and the members of the church seemed to be caught between wanting a political dialogue and wanting a religious worship service. Thus they were unable to establish a consistent liturgical framework for worship. Brown saw the changes as experimental: He reported that services were modified from year to year, always with the hope of attracting new people. Over the years they varied between a traditional religious service, with hymns, prayers, scripture readings, doxology, sermon, and benediction, and a forum situation, with a strongly secular orientation that included a brief service before the sermon and a discussion afterward. The church's letterhead called the church a temple and a forum. But it was largely upon the forum element that the reputation of the Harlem Unitarian Church was built. It drew people through the quality of its speakers and the open dialogue, yet its character as a forum also left it vulnerable to the kind of disruption described earlier. Moreover, it left some members desiring a service that was more religious in content and format.

In 1930 a Mr. Albury, a member of the Harlem church, spoke directly with Walter Hunt, the association's New York field secretary. He complained that the church was too atheistic, and that Brown and the majority had absolutely no desire for anything religious. He claimed the tendency was to make the service purely secular by relying on addresses and discussions. This left Mr. Albury and approximately twenty-five other members feeling unrepresented in the church. Hunt, who was trying to keep Brown and the church at arm's length, could offer Albury no assistance.[96]

The church continued to experiment with its pattern of worship. In 1938 when Dale DeWitt had begun working with the church, he reported:

Brown has had a rather difficult problem making a transition from the forum, which had very little organization behind it but was fairly well attended, to an organized church. Some people who were only interested in the Forum have been lost and the church attendance has not been so large.[97]

In May 1939 A. Powell Davies made this report to the association's extension committee:

The Harlem Unitarian Church lost ground, so far as attendance is concerned, when 2 years ago the nature of the service was changed, and the forums abandoned. Mr. Brown felt, mistakenly, that this was necessary in order to secure support from the American Unitarian Association.[98]

Despite Davies's criticism, Brown's change away from the forums helped to put the church on sounder organizational ground. Then services changed again: Members began to have forums once a month and eventually went back to the old style of having forums every week. Later there were still more changes, and the forum was held once a month until 1946, when the forum meetings were ended. Reflecting upon the church's constantly changing pattern of worship, Brown wrote, "In all honesty it must be recorded that this phase of our work with its changes and with our uncertainty as to what was best was the least creditable of all."[99] This wavering between a traditional worship service and a forum betrays an uncertainty in the religious self-understanding. In Brown's sense of religious purpose and in the members' statements, several unreconciled, although not unreconcilable, commitments are evident.

One of Brown's basic urges was to "emancipate [the black] from the emotionalism and superstition and other-worldliness of the old time religion."[100] Brown's beliefs, in Unitarian fashion, were stated at times in the negative, as in this description of the church that appeared in a newspaper: "It has been aptly described as a church-forum where the honey-in-heaven and harassment-in-Hades type of religion is not tolerated. There are no 'amen corners' in this church, and no 'sob sister bench.'"[101] Here are stated, as in the letter to the editor of the *Amsterdam News*, the sentiments that Brown was trying to counteract in his challenge to orthodoxy in Harlem.[102] Yet Brown was not simply a reactionary. In that same letter he called for a religion that emphasizes personal responsibility for the world, for he had formulated a positive religious viewpoint.

In a sermon entitled "Jesus of Nazareth, the World's Greatest Religious Teacher, Was a Unitarian," he wrote, "The religion of Jesus was a religion of character and service, all growing out of a personal intimate communion with God—a religion of the spirit."[103] For Brown, this religion of the spirit was manifest in service to humanity. Elsewhere, in answering a question on faith, he said, "I have faith in the inherent goodness and rightness of man; faith in the power of truth and faith in the redeeming force of a spiritual religion destined to grow from strength to strength."[104] These statements only summarize a part of Brown's religion. He was typically Unitarian in much of his theology, believing in the oneness of God, discipleship to Jesus, and the goodness of humankind. Salvation lay in character and service. He quested after truth, using all the resources available to him, both secular and biblical.

Brown's beliefs are also reflected in "The Statement of Purpose of the Harlem Unitarian Church," which reads:

> This Church is an institution of religion dedicated to the service of humanity.
>
> Seeking the truth in freedom, it strives to apply it in love for the cultivation of character, the fostering of fellowship in work and worship, and the establishment of a righteous social order which shall bring abundance of life to man.
>
> Knowing not sect, class, nation or race it welcomes each to the service of all.

In this statement there is a dual commitment to service and truth, with a single purpose: to serve humanity through the development of character. This leads one to expect Brown's sermons to fluctuate between the services that were often political and other-directed and the development of character, which would tend to be personal and spiritually inner-directed. Brown's sermons did swing back and forth between these points. In sermons like "The God I Lost, and the God I Found," "The Search for Truth," "Humanism," and "Marriage," Brown emphasized religious issues. Less frequently he preached sermons like "Police Brutality in Harlem" and "The Court Faces the People." These sermons, if explicitly political, are implicitly religious in their concern for others. Brown often left the sociopolitical topics to his guest speakers, who included individuals like Lester Granger and Roy Wilkins. Those who wished the service to have greater religious content and those who preferred a secular bent created a tension that led to a varying pattern of worship.

Despite Brown's emphasis on the intellectual and the political in religion, he did not forsake the spiritual-emotional element; the religious was not abandoned for the secular. Brown delivered an address to the Unitarian Metropolitan Conference on May 16, 1954, entitled "Making Religion More Satisfying Emotionally." There he quoted Alfred North Whitehead:

> Intellect is to the emotion as our clothes to our bodies. We could not well have civilized life without clothes, but we would be in a poor way if we had only clothes without bodies.[105]

Brown believed that emotion was central to religion, and music was one way of introducing emotion into the worship service. Music always played an important part in Brown's life. From the time he taught himself to play the piano and then taught his children, from the time he was an organist for the Methodist church until he played for his own services in Harlem, he treasured music. His sermons were peppered with words from hymns that had inspired him throughout his life. For Brown, emotion was present in music and emotion was the factor that made a sermon qualitatively different from a lecture. Knowing that this element was missing from many Unitarian churches he exhorted his Unitarian brethren to reclaim the emotional dimension of religion.

In emphasizing the emotional and spiritual in religion, Brown was caught between those who desired a worship service that was devotional and those who wanted one that was intellectual. Mr. Albury complained in 1930 that the church was too secular, and in 1938 Hodge Kirnon, a longtime chairman of the board, felt Brown put too much emphasis on worship. Brown found himself reaching out to both sides and satisfying neither. The devotional element brought in a stable group, the loyal people who pledged, and the intellectual element brought in the numbers and the notoriety.

The obstacles before the Harlem Unitarian Church, which were always great, loomed even larger in certain areas. The church never had its own space to gather in; it rented a hall or the chapel at the YWCA for a Sunday evening service. There was no other common time or space for the members. They had little success in starting a Sunday school, although one existed for several years in the late 1930s. For a time the Laymen's League had organized the forum and, of course, there were church officers, but this single-function church was an exception in the black community, where the church was traditionally the social center, the fulcrum, of black community life. The Harlem Unitarian Church must have seemed to relate only tangentially to the lives of its members and to be held together largely by the political and intellectual interests of its members. Despite Brown's pastoral endeavors, the church, by its very nature, did not address the broader human needs of its members, and this accounts for the financial situation of the church. In "A Brief History of the Harlem Unitarian Church," Brown reported the shocking fact that "in this matter of finances it may fittingly be recorded that for some reason or other the members of the church paid no regular subscription until the year begun October 1, 1935."[106] Such financial neglect indicates at least a lack of commitment. Despite Harlem's depressed economy, people contributed to whatever church was an important element in their lives. The weakness of these intellectually and politically spawned commitments was seen in the decline of membership after the church abandoned the forum format.

Who was drawn to the Harlem church? We know there were initially the left-wing radicals, many Jamaicans, but only a few black Americans. On a number of occasions Brown mentioned people who had forsaken organized religion until they found the Harlem church. The overwhelming impression is that people came for political and intellectual reasons. Large crowds gathered to hear prominent speakers like John Haynes Holmes, but since the attendance at these services was not reflected in a growing membership or budget, we must assume that the bulk of these people were not committed to the liberal gospel or to the church community. One wonders whether the situation in Harlem paralleled that in Jamaica. Bygrave reported he was impressed by the intelligence of the three hundred people who came to hear him speak. Interestingly, these were mostly young men—a group from which one is least likely to build a church community. John Lathrop made a similar observation about the makeup of the Harlem church in 1934, and, indeed, the membership rolls of the Harlem Unitarian Church show many more men than women. This church was an institutional anomaly, for church is traditionally a women's haven.

This peculiarity of membership prevented the Harlem Unitarian Church from becoming a viable religious community. By 1940 it had achieved some financial stability, and the membership had grown to fifty-three, but in 1941 the

membership suddenly dropped to twenty-three and thereafter averaged about twenty-five. What happened? There is
no institutional crisis recorded in Brown's papers, but in
August 1941, Pearl Harbor was bombed and the United
States entered the Second World War. Young men were
drafted or enlisted in the armed forces. The sharp drop in
membership may well reflect the fact that a significant
number in Brown's congregation were young men.

Although the church membership never returned to its
old level, not even after the war, Brown never seemed to
take note of this and persisted in his efforts to maintain a
temple of liberal religion in Harlem. In 1940 at the age
of sixty-five, Brown felt as if his life were just beginning.
Living on his pension, which was later augmented by an
additional four hundred dollars per year from the Society
for Ministerial Relief, he could work unhindered for the
church, and he looked forward to the future. Other people
had different ideas. There had long been an undercurrent
of doubt that Brown simply was not the right person for
the church in Harlem. This was never candidly told Brown,
and the people who expressed this opinion did so without
clarifying their comments. It is difficult to know whether
they were simply responding to his failure—from a middle-
class perspective that considers financial success the measure of a man's worth—or whether they saw something in
Brown's personality that hampered his efforts.

Other people agreed with the opinion expressed by A.
Powell Davies:

He himself is very popular. It is felt that he has not
yet had much of a chance ... My net judgment is that

> Brown is doing a pretty good job of paving the way
> for the kind of successor you will eventually be able
> to appoint.[107]

This became the hope of many, including Brown. One officer had even proposed that Brown's pension be granted
on the condition that he step aside for a younger man, but
it was clear that at age sixty-five Brown was not yet ready
to step aside. DeWitt, who was earnestly seeking a successor, hoped to avoid a competition between the new and
old ministers. The question remained, How could the Unitarian officials effect a transition? Brown forwarded one
suggestion in a letter to Everett M. Baker, the association's
executive vice-president, in March 1940 when applying for
his service pension.

> [The Harlem Unitarian Church] will continue as long
> as I am able physically and mentally to carry on . . .
> that will lie for about ten years more . . . I would . . .
> work to the end that at the time of enforced retire-
> ment it would be my great privilege to hand over
> to my successor a well established and growing
> church.[108]

Ten years was longer than DeWitt had in mind, and longer
than the likely candidates were able to wait. At the time
there were two young black ministers who could have succeeded Brown: Jeffrey Campbell was a Universalist and a
graduate of St. Lawrence; Benjamin Richardson was an
unaffiliated liberal who had graduated from Harvard Divinity School. Both had spoken at the Harlem church, and it
was thought that one of them might move into a position
as Brown's assistant. But upon his visit to the Harlem

church, Richardson "discovered that Brown had no intention of leaving."[109] Out of respect for Brown, Richardson
did not want to intrude on Brown's ministry, and he did
not see how one could move in and work with Brown. In
the absence of a building, the man himself had become the
foundation of the Harlem Unitarian Church, and Brown's
ministry to the community was not easily handed on.
White Unitarians, viewing this church from outside the
black community, did not understand the nature of
Brown's relationship to Harlem. As it turned out, the man
was irreplaceable.

The passing years did not dim Brown's hopes for the
church. An article written by Brown entitled "I Have Two
Dreams" appeared in the *Christian Register* in December
1947. The dreams he offered the denomination were of
genuine interracial churches in America and a Unitarian
church in Harlem. His was not simply wishful thinking;
Brown had already begun work on both goals.

On October 1, 1944 at the opening of the season
1944–45 it was publicly announced that the Harlem
Unitarian Church was an inter-racial church. For the
full season the white ministers of the Metropolitan
Conference preached for us on alternate Sunday
evenings and brought members of their congregations with them. The Rev. John Haynes Holmes,
Minister of the Community Church, enthusiastically
approved of what we had done and asked to be enrolled as an honorary member. The Rev. Donald Harrington, Associate Minister of the Community Church
. . . and his wife enrolled as members. We enrolled
later a white woman and man, both of whom have
since left New York. It was in many respects an inspiring and revealing season.[110]

During the previous summer, in 1944, the Reverend
Howard Thurman had become cominister of the Church
for the Fellowship of All Peoples. Located in San Francisco, this church was integrated at its inception and saw
itself as an experiment. Whether the similar experiment in
Harlem occurred as a response to this, or whether their
simultaneous emergence as interracial churches was coinci-
dental, a sign of the changing times, is not known. In any
case, the experiment in Harlem was less successful, and an
angry letter from Brown to the "Negro Religious Liberals"
appeared in the *Amsterdam News*. Brown wrote that on a
number of Sundays he had found many whites but few
blacks in attendance, and he castigated Harlem's liberals
for being so unresponsive. At the end of the 1944–1945
season the church went on as it had in previous years, but
from then on there were usually only a few white members. One Dutch immigrant was particularly involved, and
a number of other people came from Holmes's Community
Church out of a sense of duty.

A year after this season had passed a controversy arose
when Donald Szantho Harrington, Holmes's successor at
Community Church, began advertising in New York's black
newspapers. Brown saw this as unfair competition, while
Harrington claimed he was simply reaching out to the
whole city. In response to Brown's protest, which Harrington heard through DeWitt, Harrington promised Brown
that he would only advertise the Community Church's
morning service, not the evening one, in order to avoid a
conflict. It is not hard to imagine Brown's resentment
toward this large church, which, by the year of his death,
was already one-fifth black.

The attraction some blacks felt for Community Church highlights another obstacle Brown had to contend with—black racism. Prejudice within the black community went beyond the West Indian–black American conflict; it included distinctions between class and skin color. Oppressed people subconsciously accept the values of their oppressors; among blacks that has meant "white is right." Upper-class and light-skinned blacks, often the same group, preferred to attend a prestigious white religious institution like Community Church rather than listen to an old, dark Jamaican in a small YWCA chapel. The situation was not unlike the one Bygrave observed in Jamaica. Harold Cruse also reports that middle-class Jamaicans had "the deepest of skin color phobias."[111] The same is true of the American black, if perhaps to a lesser degree. This internal class and color prejudice was a factor when a group of well-known black professionals, although forming a committee to aid Brown, declined to join the church. Lamenting this, Brown wrote, "One disappointment to many of us is the indifference of the Negro professionals and of the college boys and girls of Harlem."[112]

Brown was not daunted by his limited success in creating an interracial church or by in-group prejudice. He persevered in pursuit of his second dream, building a church for his congregation in Harlem. Ironically, his own class consciousness prevented him from starting a church in a storefront, as was common practice—an unfortunate inhibition.

In January 1946 the church boldly launched a campaign to secure $15,000 to purchase a house to be transformed into a church building. The campaign

was opened with a Recital on January 27, given in All
Souls Unitarian Church . . . This was followed by a
Rally held in the Harlem YWCA on Sunday evening,
May 5. Both functions were successful. Unfortunately
the year 1947 passed without any effort in behalf of
the Building Fund. In 1948 the 1946 pattern was
followed. Again our efforts were crowned with success. The net result of these special efforts is that at
this date our Building Fund has to its credit the sum
of $1980.00. We have a long way yet to go, but when
we remind ourselves that on January 1946 we had
not a cent we are not discouraged. In fact as we start
the season of 1949-50 on this Sunday morning, September 11, 1949, we are buoyed with a strange op-
timism which emboldens us to look forward to
1950 as our year of destiny—the year in which the
corner stone of a Temple of Religious Liberalism will
be laid.[113]

The year 1950, like 1956 and every other year in Brown's
eyes, was to be the year of destiny, but it would never be
his destiny to build a church in Harlem. Year to year the
building fund grew slowly; five years later it had reached
$3,089. Earlier, in 1947, Brown had appealed to the Amer-
ican Unitarian Association for assistance, but they told
him "that under the present circumstances they did not
believe it was advisable to grant" his request.[114] The "present circumstances," which the committee did not share
with Brown, were "Mr. Brown's age . . . and the fact that
in all his years in Harlem he has never made the slightest
dent on the community and today has a very tiny group
of interested Negro Unitarians."[115]

Unknown to Brown, on another occasion, in 1950, a
Mrs. M. L. Ogan, who had earlier taken an interest in Brown

and had previously made small contributions, asked Holmes whether it would be wise to contribute three thousand dollars she had received on an insurance policy that came to term. As a way of cautioning her, Holmes wrote of Brown's years of trial and little success. Finally, he advised her that if she really understood the risk and was intent on giving, she should use the money as a grant to be matched, one that would revert to her estate if unused.

Brown's time had come and gone. A number of the larger urban churches were becoming racially integrated. In 1947 the Community Church, having begun integration prior to 1920, called a black minister of education, the Reverend Maurice Dawkins. In the same year the Reverend Lewis A. McGee began the Free Religious Fellowship, a predominantly black Unitarian church, in Chicago. Later, Benjamin Richardson became McGee's successor. When the denomination set up the Commission on Unitarian Intergroup Relations in 1952, Dr. Errold D. Collymore, a member of the Community Unitarian Church of White Plains, New York, and the Reverend Howard Thurman were its black members. Brown faded from sight and from mind. Today, many people still recall seeing him at May meetings, and some remember hearing him speak. A few knew him, but none were close enough to him to understand the drive that kept him going until he died in 1956.

Time seems to have conspired against Ethelred Brown. How could any one man, who was more often undermined than helped by the very people he turned to for support, overcome the effects of two world wars, the Great Depression, black and white racism, classism, black Christian orthodoxy, a woeful family life, and his own personal idiosyncrasies? It was too much to expect Brown to have hammered success out of this, but it was not enough to keep him from trying.

There is still one important question about his life: What drove Brown on when his hope of building a church in Harlem was threatened time and again? The trait most characteristic of Ethelred Brown was the relentlessness with which he pursued his dream. In a 1911 issue of the *Christian Register*, Brown wrote an article entitled "A Story and an Appeal" in which he recounted his early struggle to establish a Unitarian Church in Jamaica. He concluded with these words:

> The call is distinct and clear: the field is fertile and promising. Are we to heed the call and enter the field?
> By the uniqueness of the whole situation . . . by what has been attempted and done, by what is now being done, by what may be done, in the remembrance of our own inheritance, the intellectual and spiritual freedom we prize and enjoy, I make this appeal in confidence that it will call forth the response which I venture to say it deserves.[116]

Striking out on his new venture in Jamaica, Brown had been full of hope and ready to meet the future. It was to be a future that brought unexpected trials and painful failures. Yet in 1950, after almost forty years of struggle that left him with a congregation of twenty, Brown could still write John Haynes Holmes this note:

> DEAR DR. HOLMES,
> I am constrained to invite you to rejoice with us. At the close of yesterday's service we enrolled *three* members—2 young men and one young woman.

Knowing our long heart-rending history you will be able fully to appreciate why for us that was a joyful and thrilling incident.

Can it be that after years of trusting toil and patient waiting the days of harvest are at hand? Can it be? Even though I am happy I hesitate to answer even to myself. Enough is the joy of this hour.[117]

The many years of toil gave a measure of caution to his words, but the hope he held still burned brightly. What kind of a man could so tenaciously follow a dream?

There are two facets of Ethelred Brown that make his drive and his resilience understandable. He pursued laudable ideals, and yet was driven by a tragic obsession. He refused to be sentenced to a mundane life as a common laborer if it meant betraying himself and his mission so that he might live more comfortably. The mission of which he never lost sight was the delivery of liberal religion to the black community. On August 11, 1948, a short article appeared in the *New York Times* that captured a sense of Brown's values. The article was entitled "Harlem Pastor Defends Idealism," and it read, "A defense of idealism was made yesterday at the Unitarian Church of All Souls . . . by the Rev. Ethelred Brown, pastor of the Harlem Unitarian Church. As guest preacher at the morning service, Mr. Brown said that *men who visualize better days and believed that visions may become true were really 'practical.'*" For Brown these words were not mere verbiage; they proclaimed one of the principles that guided his life. The sermon was his testament.

The price for his idealism was high, his victories few, and the effect on his life almost ruinous. Brown's daughter Dorice once lamented, "We suffered more than he in our way . . . but he just didn't want to give [the mission] up."[118] The needs of Brown's family clearly seemed to be secondary to his mission. Energy that could have been used to ensure their well-being was used to advance the liberal religious cause. Brown had known his future wife, Ella, from the age of twelve and in the course of events had married her when he was twenty-three, but Brown's commitment, indeed his spiritual marriage, was to the ministry. His priorities were not so different from those of many other ministers: Family often comes second in their lives, but the conditions their families must endure are rarely so appalling as those facing Brown's family.

Brown's perspective on his personal difficulties no doubt differed sharply from that of his wife and children. He sent this song to the directors of the American Unitarian Association after they refused to reinstate him as a fellowshiped minister:

Brown suffered, but his suffering was qualitatively different from that of his family. For him, suffering and failure were not incongruous with hope and faith but rather the essence of it. Failure did not impair his sense of self-worth or subdue his high expectations. In his ministry and idealism he found a resource that sustained him through the many tragedies he knew. "The Price We Pay" was the title of one of Brown's sermons in which he alluded to Emerson's saying "There is a law of compensation *and it works.*" Brown concluded:

Choose, my friends, but know in choosing, that you shall be paid for what you have done—no more, no less; and know also that the law never changes and that to obtain the object of your choice you must always pay the price. Choose, then, my brethren, choose. What will you have? Pay the price and take it.

For Brown, his own suffering had meaning, and finding meaning in his life, he was sustained. What meaning was there for his family to discover through their suffering? Was it their cause? Their calling? Ethelred Brown, like Karl Wallenda, the high-wire artist, watched his family plummet from the tightrope that is life and then continued on himself, adamantly refusing to give up the only life he knew—indeed not knowing how to give it up.

Ethelred Brown is a very human hero, a man torn between diverging duties and driven by self-interest, too. Within the man, beside his laudable hopes there lurked a selfish zeal, a ministerial hubris that put his family's needs second. It was this hubris that kept him from giving the church over to younger hands that might have been able to sustain that community after his death. This is the tragedy. Neither the church nor his family was foremost in Brown's mind; foremost was his need to fill the ministerial role and forward his cause. In a way the extent of his suffering, to which the American Unitarian Association contributed, chained him to the ministry. He could not discount his entire life's work by forsaking the cause for which he had suffered. He was trapped both by his old pain and his ever-blossoming hope.

Brown's personality was similar to Eric Hoffer's "true believer":

> The burning conviction that we have a holy duty toward others is often a way of attaching our drowning selves to a passing raft. What looks like giving a hand is often a holding on for dear life. Take away our holy duties and you leave our lives puny and meaningless. There is no doubt that in exchanging a self-centered for a selfless life we gain enormously in self-esteem.[119]

It is probable that much of Brown's self-esteem was tied to the prestige he felt as Unitarianism's vanguard in the black community. His personal failings notwithstanding, Brown brought the message of liberal religion to Jamaica and Harlem, and was heard. Looking back over the years, he wrote:

> Our work has not failed—not failed at all. We have leavened Harlem. We have compelled many churches to soften the emphasis on the old outmoded doctrines, and, in fact, Harlem is today theologically speaking a different and a better place because we are there.[120]

He had been enlightened by liberal religion; it freed him and strengthened him with the hope that he might emancipate others. And in the end, he held to the faith to which he had dedicated his life:

When of my own free will I entered the ministry I swore to remain a minister for richer for poorer for better for worse until death. That oath I have kept for forty years. God helping me I shall keep it to the end.[121]

Lewis A. McGee

Chapter Three

A Dream Pursued:
Lewis McGee and the Free
Religious Fellowship

During the later years of Ethelred Brown's ministry in Harlem, there were other opportunities for Unitarianism to address the black community and to integrate its own ministry. In 1948 Eugene Sparrow, a black seminarian at Harvard Divinity School, was serving as the assistant minister of the Unitarian church in Somerville, Massachusetts. In the same year another black man, Maurice Dawkins, was called to the Community Church of New York to be its minister of education. It was also in 1948 that Lewis A. McGee was installed as the first minister of the Free Religious Fellowship, a predominantly black Unitarian church.

One Sunday morning early in 1947, Lewis and Marcella McGee met Harry I. Jones as all three were leaving the Chicago Ethical Society. In the ensuing conversation they expressed concern that in the great black metropolis of the South Side of Chicago, where over 275,000 blacks resided, people did not know about liberal religion. The outgrowth of their talk was a meeting of black men and women to discuss religion. Lewis McGee, one of the initiators of this discussion, was a student at Meadville Theological School at the time and would soon guide Unitarianism's second venture into black culture. Unlike Ethelred Brown, Lewis

McGee was not one to seek out controversy. Edwin H.
Wilson, who worked with Lewis on the staff of the American Humanist Association, wrote of him:

> Lewis McGee was a prince of a man, a *gentle*man in
> the finest sense of the word. He was easy to love and
> was loved by many . . . [He] had his own opinions
> and the strength to move from an inherited faith for
> whose ministry he had trained, to a liberal religious
> viewpoint. He had a warm, non-aggressive way about
> him that won respect and friendship. His "chuckly"
> sense of humor, often visibly repressed, was one mark
> of his love of life.

Lewis was fifty-four when he entered Meadville, and the
odyssey that had led him to Unitarianism had been a long
one. Born on November 11, 1893, in Scranton, Pennsyl-
vania, Lewis was virtually born into the ministry. His father,
a former slave, was an African Methodist Episcopal (AME)
minister. As a local pastor and then a district supervisor,
his father was moved from post to post by the bishop.[1]
Lewis graduated from high school in 1912. He spent one
year at the University of Pittsburgh and then continued his
education at the Payne Theological Seminary of Wilber-
force University in Ohio, from which he graduated in 1916
with a B.D. A year later he was ordained as an elder in the
AME church.

Just as McGee was an AME minister before he became
a Unitarian, Brown, a Wesleyan Methodist, was attracted to
the AME church before he made his decision to become
a Unitarian minister. This initial attraction to the AME
church is significant. A relatively privileged class of blacks,
the aspiring lower middle class, were members of the black

Methodist churches. Among these, "the AME showed continuing concern for higher education without sacrificing its commitment to spirituality."[2] The AME's concerns reflect the change in the world view of its members that accompanies increasing education and economic self-sufficiency. Brown and McGee are typical examples of the educated and middle-class church members drawn to the AME church and Unitarianism. Both denominations share middle-class values, and it is therefore easier to move between Methodism and Unitarianism than between some other religions.

In 1918 Lewis joined the Ninety-second Infantry Division of the U.S. Army as a chaplain. After his discharge, he ministered to a succession of AME churches in Ohio and West Virginia. These were small churches, and as was often the case among black ministers, Lewis worked at another job to support his family. McGee, like Brown, first became aware of Unitarianism by accident. Lewis recalled the events around 1920, when he was ministering to an AME church in Collinwood, Ohio, outside Cleveland.

I found it necessary to supplement my meager misson salary by being a mail carrier for Uncle Sam. One day, in the mail on my desk for delivery, I saw a magazine entitled the *Christian Register.* The word Christian caught my attention and I opened it and glanced at the headings of the articles. I delayed delivery for a couple of days in order to read the contents. I liked it.

Then my good Methodist conscience took over and at the delivery I rang the doorbell and made my confession. The lady of the house, a good Unitarian, answered, "Why, help yourself, read it all you want. I invite you to visit our church down on Euclid Avenue." At the first opportunity I did visit the Sunday

> morning service. There was a quiet pervading the at-
> mosphere. The hymns and readings were appealing.
> The sermon inspiring. I don't remember a word that
> was said but I was very much impressed and had a
> strong feeling, "This is the kind of church I would
> like to minister to." I guess I was one of those Uni-
> tarians who did not know it.[3]

McGee liked what he considered the worshipful attitude of
the congregation, and he appreciated the "dignity" with
which the service was held, because he had never been comfortable appealing to his parishioners' emotions. McGee's encounter with Unitarianism served to reinforce ideas he had
developed in theological school, where he had been critical
of traditional, dogmatic religion. Lewis continued on as an
AME minister, albeit a skeptical one. The question now before him was how to act upon this new discovery.

In 1927 McGee journeyed to Chicago, where he met the
Unitarian minister Curtis Reese, who had edited a collection of sermons, entitled *Humanist Sermons*, that set forth
the principles of humanism. McGee read this collection
and decided he too was a humanist. Five years later, in
1933, Curtis Reese, along with John Dewey and others,
signed the controversial Humanist Manifesto, which expressed clearly the principles of this group. Humanism was
and is an effort to challenge the identification of religion
with doctrines and methods that do not address the problems of the twentieth century, dogmas that could not be
reconciled with a scientific view of the world. It views the
universe as self-existing and not created; furthermore, it
holds humanity to be a part of nature that developed as
part of the natural process, not by divine creation. Humanism places the responsibility for shaping civilization squarely

upon the individual. The manifesto also voiced a dissatisfaction with the profit-making orientation and envisioned
the establishment of a cooperative economic order. In its
time this declaration was vehemently attacked within the
American Unitarian Association, not to mention the larger
society. It was not a movement one joined casually. Nevertheless, McGee joined with the Humanists and in addition
approached Reese about entering the Unitarian ministry.
Reese candidly told him, "If you want to become a Unitarian minister, you'll have to bring your own church." In
1927 it was still out of the question for a black man to
minister to a white church.

Lewis bided his time. He remained in Chicago and accepted a position as a social worker for the Illinois Children's Home and Aid Society. Subsequently, he worked for
a number of other social welfare agencies. While he was
working, he took courses at the University of Chicago and
Loyola University, and in 1936 he received a B.A. in social
science from Carthage College in Carthage, Illinois. After
graduation Lewis ministered to a church in Iowa for two
years and then returned to Chicago, where he continued to
work and minister to a succession of churches there and in
Gary, Indiana. Still he had not forsaken his newfound
faith. In 1941 he began a decade of service on the board of
the American Humanist Association. It is hard to imagine
how he managed to do this while also serving a Christian
church, and we can only assume he did not announce it
from the pulpit.

In 1943 Lewis reenlisted as a chaplain in the U.S. Army
and soon found himself with the Ninety-fifth Infantry Division in Belgium. His experiences in World War II brought
him to a religious crisis. As he lay in his cot listening to the

bombs flying overhead, he wondered why he should risk
his life for his country but not give his life in service to his
ideals. He came home feeling that his life would be less
than lived if he did not have access to a free pulpit. Moreover, he witnessed the beginnings of the integration of
American troops during the last stages of the war.[4] After
seeing this, Lewis felt that there was no reason that the
church could not be integrated as well.

After serving in France, Wales, England, Belgium, and
Germany, McGee left the army in the autumn of 1945 with
the rank of captain, and immediately married Marcella;
it was a second marriage for both. With the war over and
a new marriage, McGee faced the question of how best to
pursue the convictions that had been awakened. His options
were presented in the report of an interview with one of
the faculty members of the Meadville Theological School:

[A] man of apparently established and solid worth. I
was very much attracted to him. He seemed to know
precisely where he was, and where he wanted to go.
He also seemed to me to be widely educated and [of
a] thoroughly liberal personality. He gives the distinct
impression of ability and stability.

The possibilities which lie before him are (1) to remain within the African Methodist Church and continue a process of liberalism (the difficulty here lies
in the fact that he has to suppress his own convictions
to change); (2) establish a brand new liberal movement among his own people in Chicago or some
other city (this would require financial backing);
(3) find a colored, liberal church to which he could
go (e.g. Ethelred Brown's in Harlem); (4) associate
himself with some established liberal church and
help to make it inter-racial. The whole matter was

left in abeyance for the time being to see what would develop.[5]

The fact that the AME bishop did not settle him or any of the other ministers he had promised to reassign when they returned from the service helped Lewis to make a decision. In September 1946 he entered Meadville to prepare himself to be fellowshiped as a Unitarian.

While traveling in the summer before class started, he and Marcella stopped to visit the Reverend Everett M. Baker, minister of the First Unitarian Church of Cleveland. Later Baker wrote to Wallace Robbins, the president of Meadville, that he had been favorably impressed by the couple, but "I did not encourage him to think that there is much opportunity for a Negro minister in our fellowship."[6] The question of placing Lewis McGee remained, despite a change in the church. Lewis felt, with good reason, that he had Robbins's support. Yet Robbins was honest about his chances: "I told him that because of his age and race the prospects would be very slight. He accepted that judgment [and] entered whole-heartedly into the life of the school."[7] Robbins held out the hope to McGee that they could secure him a position as an assistant or associate in a large urban church.

Robbins worked to find him a job. When he heard that the Universalist Church in America had a position, he wrote its president, Robert Cummins, about McGee's skills as a minister and social worker. Cummins replied that he was interested: "We have had splendid work for Negroes in Suffolk, Virginia. It is now modernized. We are proud of it—a social service project. A grand opportunity for a church there, and it is this that I have in mind."[8] Cummins was describing here an institution that the black Universalist minister Joseph F. Jordan had ministered to at the beginning of the century. McGee never followed up on this possibility. He was committed to Unitarianism, and, besides, the Free Religious Association (later changed to the Free Religious Fellowship) was beginning to take shape.

The Free Religious Fellowship (FRF) had begun with that chance meeting of the McGees and Harry Jones outside the Ethical Society. Jones had suggested that a group of people interested in liberal religion

> meet at his home for a general discussion. Three such informal meetings were the result, out of which grew the plan to hold regular meetings at a more public place. One of the large rooms at Abraham Lincoln Center, 700 E. Oakwood, was secured and five meetings were held in the Spring, at 4 P.M. on the second and fourth Sundays of April and May, and the third Sunday of June 1947. A mailing list was prepared, notices sent out announcing the topics for discussion and some twenty different persons attended one or more meetings.
>
> The topics presented, in order, were "Why Make a New Approach to Religion," "The Liberal Way in Religion," "Liberalism Faces a Hostile World," "What Is Unitarianism" and "Free, for What?" In each case [McGee] led off with a twenty minute talk and then asked for questions or discussions. These gatherings were marked by a growing interest which became more and more sharply defined toward the possibility of a Unitarian Fellowship.[9]

When Lewis McGee found that people were interested in the liberal religious perspective, he approached Wallace

Robbins and Randall Hilton, the secretary of the Western Unitarian Conference, with the idea of a survey of black Chicagoans: "Feeling the challenge as I do, I am writing you to help me find the answer to a direct question. It is this: 'What is the Unitarian Church prepared to do in response to this challenge?' "[10] In response to McGee's letter, Robbins wrote to George Davis of the Department of Unitarian Extension and Church Maintenance, who replied that he had already spoken to Hilton and that the project should be undertaken.[11]

The American Unitarian Association was clearly more responsive to McGee than it had been to Brown, and we cannot avoid asking why. Primarily, the association's behavior was due to the simple fact that times had changed and the denomination had been actively looking for ways of addressing the black community. Brown had been receiving support for ten years, but given his long, fruitless effort in Harlem, the denomination was not inclined to invest more money in Brown's enterprise. Lewis McGee offered the fresh start the association officers were looking for.

McGee was hired by the association to survey the black community of Chicago's South Side to determine whether or not there was any potential for a black Unitarian church. This was the second time such a survey had been proposed. In 1945 the Chicago Unitarian Council had made a similar proposal for a survey that was never carried out. Another black Meadville student, Alvin Neely Cannon, was to conduct the survey, but the faculty expressed strong reservations about him. In general, they found him to be a personable but unwilling student. Robbins and others were concerned that the first attempt to address Chicago's black community not fail, and that would be the risk with Cannon. They also questioned the advisability of the surveyor's becoming the first minister. This reservation should have applied to McGee as well as to Cannon, for it put pressure on the surveyor not only to determine but also to prove the viability of a church. In one sense, a report by McGee or anyone else was unnecessary, because even as McGee began his research, the group that had gathered earlier at Harry Jones's home was gaining momentum. The existence of this group, in the end, was the strongest argument for establishing a church. Still, the fact that a study was commissioned set McGee apart from Brown. Brown marched into Harlem to found his church regardless of the circumstances; McGee had the foresight to look before he leaped and to know that a substantial report would help to legitimize denominational support.

The momentum the FRF gained in that first year was due to the energies of a core group of people. Marcella McGee's family was well established in Chicago; they were also members of the church and had many connections. Marcella made various contacts through her job as a librarian at a branch of the public library housed in the Abraham Lincoln Center, and a number of people from the center were among the early members. Harry I. Jones was also a central figure in the formation of the FRF, for in addition to organizing the initial meetings, Jones knew many people through his community and political activities. These early members developed a mailing list and then called on their friends personally. William Gough, another member, recalls that Jones and George Walker, Marcella's brother, had visited him to invite him to join the group. He and his wife, Geneva, went once but were not impressed. The following Sunday they did not attend, but again Jones and Walker visited to tell them that on the coming Sunday Kenneth Patton would speak. Mr. Gough had heard of Patton, who had won some notoriety in the black community. On October 5, 1947, the Reverend Kenneth L. Patton, minister of the Unitarian Church of Madison, Wisconsin, spoke at what was the first regular Sunday meeting of the Free Religious Fellowship; 125 people attended, and the Goughs, after hearing his sermon "One Race, One World," decided to join.[12]

Patton's activities just prior to and following his address to the FRF give a sense of the racial climate across the country as well as in the denomination in 1947. Earlier that autumn, before speaking to the FRF, Patton, "after quietly delivering a radio talk on the subject of the 'myth of race,' suddenly found [himself] on the front pages of the nation's press." His comment that he intended to "resign from the white race" caught the public's ear, and he was dazed by the ensuing reaction. The response Patton received from his radio talk was overwhelmingly supportive, but the one letter in eight that was antagonistic "reveal[ed] the bitterness and danger of racism in America."[13] These few felt threatened and betrayed by what Patton had said. Some threatened him, and the fear-induced distortions that confronted Patton from the minds of these racists were disturbing.

Patton's radio talk led to his further involvement in the cause of racial justice. He was invited to tour Chicago with a photographer and journalist from *Life* magazine and a black couple. They tried to enter YMCAs, hotels, restaurants, and dance halls. At some places they were all admitted. At others, Patton was admitted only to find the black couple, who entered separately, had been stopped at the door; when he protested, all three were ejected. On several other occasions he would gain entry to an establishment and then announce that he was a Negro, at which point he was immediately ushered out. Patton also went to a real estate office and was offered a wide assortment of homes until he announced that he was a Negro. The homes were suddenly unavailable, and they gave him the address of another agency.

The whirlwind of activity started by his radio talk and address to the Free Religious Fellowship continued. Ten days after Patton spoke to the FRF, he was scheduled to attend the American Unitarian Association's general conference in Washington, D.C. Donald Harrington had arranged with Homer Jack, the national secretary of the Unitarian Fellowship for Social Justice, to challenge the racial policies of the Mayflower, one of the hotels the association was using, by having Ethelred Brown reserve a room there. He was to room with Kenneth Patton, but a fortnight before the conference was to begin, Brown had a change of heart. He wrote:

DEAR MR. HARRINGTON,

I appreciate your confidence in me that I would not hesitate to suffer personal embarrassment if by so doing I would help to strengthen the hands of others who aim to remedy a wrong, but after serious consideration of your suggestion a big question mark arises in my mind.

Facing a few of the possible back-fires and the fact that the suggested personal illustration is not necessary to add force to any protest or anti-segregation resolution I have come to the conclusion that the proposal is, to say the least, of questionable value. Therefore, I have decided not to attend the conference.[14]

Instead of the officers' planned confrontation, a resolution was submitted by James Luther Adams and Homer Jack that called upon Congress to enact civil rights statutes in the District of Columbia and declared the association's intention not to meet in the nation's capital until racial segregation there had ceased.

Patton's story is important for the main story line for two reasons. First, Patton's experiences illustrate the degree of racial discrimination that existed in America in the 1940s. Jim Crow was slowly losing ground. Blacks were pushing against the barriers of racism, and some Unitarians were in the forefront of the struggle with them. The way was being prepared for the stronger confrontations that were to come in the 1950s. Second, knowing about Brown's concern for social justice and his tendency to charge into the most difficult situations, I am perplexed by his refusal to join in the effort in Washington, D.C. The reasoning in his letter seems particularly vague, and I wonder what was left unsaid. Is it that he feels they would be using him? There is a caution there that one would expect to find in McGee rather than in Brown. McGee's gradual approach to Unitarianism, the exploratory meetings before the FRF was formed, and his report on the climate for liberal religion in Chicago's black community show he was a cautious and thoughtful man. Robbins once described him in a letter to George Davis as "a steady methodical person, without ecstatic visions and ultra-radical enthusiasms."[15]

This is not to say that Lewis McGee was without emotion or conviction. In the letter in which he proposed the survey to Robbins he wrote, "There is no [black] liberal church; I think there ought to be one."[16] Looking toward fulfillment of what was then only a hope, McGee's report concluded:

> The Negro community on Chicago's South Side is now the home of approximately 275,000 or more people; there are large numbers of educated, cultured and prosperous people, many of whom can be considered as candidates for a liberal church; as the churches are classified at present, there is room in the community for a Unitarian church.
>
> In addition, the Free Religious Fellowship has a record over the past three months of growth and vitality which gives promise of being such a church in embryo.
>
> It seems that if the desire and the will and the energy which the task calls for are supplied, outstanding results will be achieved.[17]

While McGee was writing this study, the FRF continued to gain momentum:

> By April 1, 1948, fifty persons or families had pledged to become members of an interracial Unitarian Church. On Sunday, April 25, 1948, the Rev. Randall S. Hilton, Secretary of the Western Unitarian Conference, presided at the official organization of the Free Religious Fellowship (Unitarian). In addition to the Rev. Hilton, the committee which represented the American Unitarian Association in supervising the work previous to the organization was composed of Dr. James Luther Adams, Professor of Social Ethics, Meadville Theological School. [Finally] on June 13, 1948, the Rev. Lewis A. McGee was installed as minister. The members of the first Board of Trustees were: Harry I. Jones, President; George Walker, Jr., Vice President; Mrs. Deborah Smith, Sec.-Treas.;

Harry L. Manley, Haywood C. Philips, Mrs. Osbeth Adams, Mrs. Charlotte Charnock, John Forwalter, Mrs. Hazel Dingey.[18]

When Lewis McGee accepted the call to be minister of the FRF, his position was different from what Brown's had been at a comparable stage in his career. Lewis's children were grown and self-sufficient, as was Marcella's daughter. Marcella's income as a librarian enabled Lewis to work at the small salary the church provided without being impoverished. Moreover, from the beginning of this endeavor he had the denomination's support. He did not have to waste his time and efforts struggling with the American Unitarian Association. McGee also lived in a different era. Racial barriers were slowly breaking down and blacks had made economic gains during the war. Brown still hoped for the future of his church and was mounting a building campaign in Harlem, but in Chicago the association had found a fresh, new hope.

With McGee as their minister, the members of the FRF set out to increase the group's membership. The congregation received publicity in the *Chicago Defender*, the major black newspaper, and in the *Chicago Sun-Times*. Now it decided to try something daring by contracting to bring the then famous One World Ensemble from New York City to Chicago. The Ensemble comprised a Japanese-American soprano, a Scotch-Irish contralto, a black American tenor, and an Anglo-American basso-cantante. They combined artistic and cultural resources into a musical symbol of world harmony, and their repertoire encompassed the music of the world. The other churches in the Chicago area helped the FRF by selling tickets to the concert. It was a daring endeavor and brought needed publicity, but it was also costly. The FRF did not fill Orchestra Hall and in the end ran a deficit of one hundred dollars.

As the membership grew and the group's programs expanded, the FRF sought new quarters. In the beginning, the group had met in people's homes. Later, they had rented space successively at Poro House, the YWCA at Forty-third Street and South Parkway, and the South Side Art Center. During these years the church membership grew from sixty-seven to ninety-eight. They had a viable Sunday school with four teachers and twenty-five pupils, an Evening Alliance, and a Laymen's League that sponsored a monthly dinner and forum. In 1951 the FRF decided to move to the Abraham Lincoln Center because it met their need for more and permanent space, but when they moved, there was an unexpected reaction: Fifty-three people dropped their membership in the FRF, and although twelve joined, this left a drastically reduced membership of fifty-seven. Something about the move to Lincoln Center precipitated a flight of FRF members. William Gough, a longtime member, speculates that the reason for this exodus from the fellowship was confusion over the center's name. The United States was in the midst of the "red scare": the FBI was combing the South Side, investigating alleged black involvement in the Communist party. In the Loop the Abraham Lincoln School served as a public forum, offering classes in politics, literature, and other subjects; a number of its teachers were Marxists. Gough conjectures that, given the climate of the time, people confused the Abraham Lincoln Center with the Abraham Lincoln School and therefore thought the church was moving into a communist hotbed.[19] In fact, unknown to McGee, inquiries were made at the main offices of the American Unitarian Association by an Illinois state official trying to determine if McGee was a communist.[20] He was not, but there were political radicals who helped found that church. The fact that Harry Jones and Jesse Reed, another FRF member, were socialists may also have contributed to this confusion over the Abraham Lincoln Center. This involvement of members of both the FRF and the Harlem Unitarian Church in socialism is another significant parallel. These independent facts begin to form a pattern when we consider that Jeffrey Campbell, a black Universalist Unitarian minister, was also a socialist and ran for governor of Massachusetts in 1938 on the Socialist ticket.

Not every departing member was concerned with radical politics. Ironically, a few members left when they moved into the Abraham Lincoln Center because they found it too churchlike. The FRF met in the auditorium of the center, which had been the home of the All Souls Church founded by Jenkin Lloyd Jones. In the Abraham Lincoln Center, built in 1905, Jones's dream of a great community center with an interracial, nonsectarian church at its heart came into being, but the church, All Souls, died in the years of the depression. Curtis Reese, now the dean of the center, had revived services at All Souls and had succeeded in integrating the church, but as the population of the neighborhood changed, attendance dwindled. The revived services finally ended in the early 1940s, because the center, which received financial aid from the Community Fund, had to distinguish those funds that went to secular activities from those that went to sustaining the church. Now that the FRF had taken over the old home of All Souls, it would eventually take on its name as well. The center had rooms for Sunday school, for storage, and for meetings during the week. Members could worship in the auditorium, with its organ and churchlike atmosphere, but the small group that gathered there was lost in the cavernous room.

One of the important goals of the FRF, from its inception, was the development of an interracial church. Most of the members were black, but the group always had some white members and, for a time, Japanese members as well. Some of the white members were Meadville students. The most active of these were Mary Cleary (née) Gibson, who was later ordained by the FRF, Hugo Leaming, who had earlier been a member of the Harlem Unitarian Church and later became a minister of the FRF, and Emil Gudmundson. There were other whites who attended services, and a number came from the First Unitarian Church of Chicago. Some felt pulled between the two churches; others gave the FRF their full commitment.

The efforts of the black Unitarian churches to become integrated and the commitment of individuals like Brown and McGee are better grasped if we examine the question of church integration from a different perspective. The efforts of the First Unitarian Church of Chicago to become integrated are especially interesting because of the church's close relationship to the FRF. The Reverend Leslie Pennington had long been involved in race relations and had frequently exchanged pulpits with black ministers in Chicago, but Pennington, though wanting an integrated church, "did not feel justified in going out deliberately to find Negroes who would consent to join a Unitarian Church."[21] In 1947 the recruiting of blacks to come "and teach brotherhood to our people," as John Haynes Holmes had done when he was on the board of the NAACP in 1909, was considered tokenism.[22] For Pennington, it was understood that blacks were welcome, but others wanted a distinct proclamation. The Evening Alliance, which included Muriel Hayward, Gladys Hilton, Margret Adams, and Dorothy Schaad, pushed for a church resolution that would clearly state that the First Unitarian Church welcomed people of all races. They knew that " 'whites only' was never carved over the door of any white Protestant church in America; it was understood."[23] To dispel this assumption, they needed to make a public statement to the contrary, but this was not an easy matter, since there were people in the congregation who opposed integration altogether. James Luther Adams remembers a meeting of the board of trustees that went late into the night as they argued over whether or not to become an integrated church. Finally, in the early hours of the morning, one trustee, still recalcitrant on the issue of integration, was challenged with this question: "What is the purpose of the church?" He blurted out, "To change people like me!" He and another trustee later left the church. In January 1948 a resolution was passed at the annual meeting, and in that year the church received its first black member. Since then it has turned into one of the most thoroughly integrated churches within the liberal faith, and this transformation was occurring at the same time the FRF was struggling to become a viable institution.

Randall Hilton, then executive director of the Western Unitarian Conference, recalls that McGee and Pennington at one time discussed the possibility of merging, but the idea never bore fruit for several reasons. First, Pennington was a theist, while McGee was a humanist.[24] Second, the two churches appealed to different constituencies. The First Unitarian Church was an upper middle class church in a university community, and many members of the FRF did not feel comfortable with the elitism and unspoken racism that naturally remained long after the resolution on integration was passed. Indeed, some members of the FRF passed by the church on their way to gather in the congenial atmosphere of the fellowship. Third, in addition to this tension, there were differences in purpose because of the fellowship's sense of mission. Fern Gayten expressed it this way: "We had an obligation to stay where we were and cast down our bucket."[25]

Casting its bucket into the black community was one of the FRF's main goals. The church tried to attract lower-class blacks, but it generally drew in educated people; most members had attended college and a significant number had attended graduate school. Church members were postal clerks, social workers, housewives, teachers, doctors, railroad employees, a radio announcer, a parole officer, a secretary, and a lawyer. (Obviously, education did not always guarantee a good job for blacks.) Still, these people formed the black middle class, a group to which Unitarianism appealed. They were people experiencing some economic autonomy, moving toward a religion that focused on the worth of the individual.

Most of these individuals had been reared within Christian orthodoxy; the largest group originally came from the African Methodist Episcopal church or other Methodist churches. These people left the orthodox faith when they found that science raised issues their churches did not answer and that the church could not give an adequate explanation for the oppression of black people. These blacks were ready to hear the humanist perspective McGee offered, and sought a community that would assist the inquiring mind. Moreover, these were people whose lives were no longer confined to the black community. Their broadening outlook required a religion that supported their quest but did not confine them as orthodoxy had. They were committed, but also valued their lives outside the church—their diverse occupations, social action, and cultural involvements. Members used their money for other priorities, too—children's education, civic organization, concerts, and so forth. To these people, "church did not have to mean as much" as it did to their orthodox brethren. For some of them, "a church that was less highly organized was acceptable," and for others, it was desirable.[26]

The involvement of FRF members in the Socialist party is an example of the broad kind of commitments that many church members made. Social action was a concern of the FRF, but it did not dominate the church as it often had in Harlem. Lewis McGee believed that religious commitment necessitates social action, but its pursuit was not all-encompassing as it was with Brown. McGee was a member of the American Civil Liberties Union, the NAACP, and the Independent Voters of Illinois, and was vice-president of his local community organization; in later years he would join the civil rights march on Selma, Alabama. He was involved, but his style was more subdued than was Brown's. This may reflect a difference between the outlook of the West Indian and that of the black American. Harold Cruse speculates that this difference is due in part to the majority status of the former in Jamaica and the minority status of the black in the United States.[27] McGee had felt the weight of Jim Crow policies throughout his life—"separate but equal education," segregated army regiments, and housing discrimination. He knew how vulnerable blacks were in America, and how accommodating they often needed to be just to survive. By contrast, Brown was not confronted with American racism until he was an adult. Where Brown felt free to assert his ideas and demands, McGee felt constrained to work quietly and consistently within viable organizations.

The Sunday morning service, which was the center of the FRF's church life, was much less elaborate than that of traditional black churches, or for that matter most Unitarian societies. Emil Gudmundson, who was widely traveled as a Unitarian Universalist Association Interdistrict Representative, remembered the services as being "closer to my experience at the Ethical Society than any Unitarian church." The service was simple: hymns, readings, announcements, collection, and sermon. It was followed by a coffee hour at which people would informally discuss the sermon. Lewis McGee was thoroughly humanistic in the content of his sermons. He preached on a variety of subjects of secular, religious, and social concern, and avoided orthodox terminology. His humanism can be seen in sermon titles like "Have Faith in Man" and "We Choose Our Destiny." The centrality of humanism to McGee's theology is clear in a sermon entitled "A Positive View of Liberal Religion":

Rejecting the idea of an infallible revelation of truth in religion placed [humanists] in the position of trusting the use of reason and conscience. Rejecting salvation through faith in a God-man Savior, the Christ, they affirmed salvation through character and by ethical living. These affirmations enabled them to pronounce judgment on rituals and practices and beliefs coming out of the past but no longer relevant to the needs and aspirations of growing life. They distinguished the accidental and particular from the permanent and the universal. With the free play of mind they laid hold of the materials about them in a serious effort to clarify and purify religious ideals and goals. On the basis of this heritage, what do Unitarians believe? We believe in individual freedom of mind, heart and conscience. We believe in the supreme value of the human person. We believe in the use of reason in religion. We believe in a welcome appreciation of difference of view in religion as in other phases of life. We believe in the human capacity to solve individual and social problems and thus to make progress. We believe in a continuing search for truth and hence that life is an adventurous quest. We believe in the scientific method as valid in ascertaining factual knowledge. We believe in the democratic process in our human relations. We believe in ethical conduct. We believe in a dynamic universe, the evolution of life, the oneness of the human family and the unity of life with the material universe. We believe in religion as [an] intellectual, emotional and volitional response to the universe, the universe of inanimate nature and the universe of life. We believe in the creative imagination as a power in promoting the good life. We believe in the creative power of love or good will in family and social relationships. We believe in action that puts into daily practice these beliefs. We believe in things beautiful as well as things good and true. We believe that religion is as broad as life and that the arts should have proper place in our celebrations. Holding these beliefs we affirm that our churches and fellow-ships are means, are necessary means, to give us sup-port, to inspire and encourage us as we remember the words of Parrington "that the promise of the future has lain always in the keeping of liberal minds that were never discouraged from their dreams."[28]

A visitor after one service was heard to say, "I don't even feel as if I've been to church."[29] The FRF was indeed a radical departure from black orthodoxy.

One would not have heard a pronouncement like McGee's from any other black pulpit in Chicago; else-where, meaning was found through one's relationship to God. Lewis's sermons were well reasoned, intellectual in content, and practical in intent; his style was restrained. Ida Cress said, "I can't conceive of Lewis getting ex-treme."[30] There was certainly no shouting at the FRF. In and out of the pulpit, Lewis was a quiet and caring man. If people did not throng to the FRF, it was in part because McGee, like Brown, was not charismatic. Fern Gayten, re-flecting upon the difference between the ministers of the FRF and those of the more orthodox congregations, said, "The kind of men who have been our leaders are not the kind of men who of themselves demand that kind of com-plete self-devotion. Our ministers have not demanded all our money or all of ourselves."[31]

By June 1953, two years after moving to the Abraham Lincoln Center, McGee had built the membership rolls up to seventy-five, and the fellowship's program was run-ning smoothly. The time had come to depart, to make room for a younger man. Lewis was sixty years old and had borne the financial sacrifice of ministering to a small

congregation for six years. He had established the idea of
the fellowship and now felt the church was strong enough
to grow with a good successor. There were several possible
candidates at the time. The primary one was the Reverend
Maurice A. Dawkins, who was the minister of education at
the Community Church in New York City, but he turned
down the offer and in 1954 was called to the Peoples Independent Church of Los Angeles, which was said to be
the oldest and second largest Community Church in the
United States.[32] Meanwhile Eugene Sparrow had graduated with his S.T.B. from Harvard in 1949. After witnessing the hedging and foot dragging of Unitarian officials,
he despaired of finding a settlement and quickly accepted
a teaching position first at Texas College and later at Jarvis
Christian College. The possibilities that had been present in
1948 had by now languished. The Unitarian denomination,
with no substantial black churches, unwilling and unable
to place black men in white pulpits, found it difficult to
attract and keep black ministers. The few who were interested quickly perceived that their own welfare demanded that they look elsewhere. Finally, in June 1954,
Benjamin Richardson, who had been viewed as a possible
successor to Brown, was called to the FRF.

McGee now faced the same problem: where could a
black minister in a white denomination find employment?
When Lewis left the FRF in 1953, he went to Yellow
Springs, Ohio to become the administrative assistant of
the American Humanist Association. There his main duty
was to serve as liaison with humanist groups and chapters.
In 1956 an opportunity for settlement arose when the
Congregational Unitarian Church of Flint, Michigan, asked

him to be a candidate for its ministry. The church and
McGee appeared to be well suited to each other. At least
five black families were attending the church, many of its
members belonged to the NAACP and the Urban League,
and the church had been instrumental in organizing the
Human Rights Commission in Flint. People were hospi-
table and the candidates' week of visits went well, but in
the end McGee did not receive the required number of
votes to be called. Why?

Those who were involved tell different stories and thus
no single reason stands out. Virginia Jordan, a member of
the Flint church who knew Marcella McGee, had originally
only suggested that Lewis come and speak. It was after he
was well received that church members decided to consider
him a candidate. Later, because of this circumstance, some
church members felt his coming had been handled in a
"devious way."[33] A second reason concerned the particular makeup of the Flint church. In 1937 the Congregational and the Unitarian churches had merged, and some
Unitarians blamed the Congregationalists for the failure to
call McGee. It is said that seldom-seen Congregationalists,
who were generally more conservative than the Unitarians,
turned out for the vote.[34] The ostensible reason was the
church's incompatibility with his humanism. Curiously, the
issue of race did not come up, even though to call McGee
would have been a truly radical step. But neither could
those who presumably were uncomfortable with if not opposed to this move speak up for fear of appearing racist.
What was felt but unsaid we cannot know. Moreover, all
these issues intermingled with the prevalent anxiety of the
McCarthy era, in which the liberal church was viewed by
many as a nest of communists, and informants did in fact

attend many meetings held at the Flint church.[35] It should be also noted that the Unitarians and the Congregationalists went their separate ways within several years of this incident. McGee wrote afterward in a letter, "I failed to get the call to Flint. The constitution requires a two thirds vote. I think I was not cautious enough in speaking my mind on a local hot potato social issue. May be a blessing in disguise."[36]

Another two years went by before McGee became Stephen Fritchman's associate minister at the First Unitarian Church of Los Angeles. The year 1958 was also the year that the First Unitarian Church of Providence, Rhode Island, called another black, William R. Jones, as assistant minister. In 1961 McGee became the first minister of the Chico Unitarian Fellowship in California. This was the first time a black man had been called as the senior minister of a white Unitarian church. In 1962 McGee was the interim minister at the Anaheim Unitarian Church. In 1963 he came out of retirement at the urging of the Throop Memorial Church in Pasadena to become their minister of education. In 1965 he was installed as the first minister at the Humboldt Unitarian Fellowship in Bayside, California, retired again, and became minister emeritus in August 1966. Lewis Allen McGee died in Pullman, Washington, on October 10, 1979, at the age of eighty-five.

Lewis McGee responded to the call to take Unitarianism into the black community. Although he and Ethelred Brown hardly knew one another, they shared this mission. Lewis's last words in the FRF newsletter were these:

I request that the members of the Free Religious Fellowship give vital, active expression of their loyalty to the organization. To each I say, fortify your belief in it, attend meetings faithfully, support your elected officers, and rally to your minister. Several times recently I have been asked this question, "What of the future of the Free Religious Fellowship?" I have answered hopefully. No one is able to chart the future definitely, but of one thing I am sure. Fifty or more loyal members *can assure that there will be a future* and they will be the prime factor in shaping the future. Don't allow doubters and those easily discouraged to influence you!

The foundation of the church is an active membership . . . I challenge you to continue to make history.[37]

Lewis McGee was different from Ethelred Brown in many ways. Perhaps most importantly Lewis was able to let go of his church when the time was right. He had come to Chicago, initiated and nurtured the Free Religious Fellowship in cooperation with others, and left it in the hands of its members while he moved on to other things. That institution lives on today in Chicago's South Side, while the church in Harlem is only a memory.

Lewis A. McGee, Dana Greeley, Stephen Fritchman

Chapter Four

How "Open" Was the Door?

Religious conviction is a powerful, sometimes over-powering, force in the life of an individual. This was certainly true for Ethelred Brown and Lewis McGee. Their lifework is a legacy of the encounter of two traditions—the black and the Unitarian—an encounter defined in part by the dynamics of intellectual, political, and spiritual freedom. Thus far I have tried to present the message they brought to the black community as they struggled to live up to their religious convictions. With this as background, I return to two questions raised earlier: First, why has de facto racial segregation persisted within the Unitarian church? Or, how "open" is the Unitarian door? And second, why did Brown's and McGee's efforts at establishing Unitarian churches in the black community flounder? Let us begin with the question of racial segregation.

What was the American Unitarian Association's response to black Unitarians? The different experiences Brown and McGee had with the association reflect the changes that took place over the first half of this century. In 1907 when Brown wrote to inquire about theological school and financial aid, denominational officials discouraged him. Unitarianism was associated with intellectual culture, and many Unitarians feared that their system of belief might be corrupted if embraced by the mass of common men and women, much less by blacks. Earl Morse Wilbur reported that in 1860 "the Secretary of the Association complained that Boston Unitarians saw no reason for diffusing their faith, and it was reported that they did not wish to make Unitarianism too common."[1] Unitarian missionary efforts were halfhearted and often patronizing. Samuel A. Eliot made great efforts to promote liberal religion, but he was highly selective: University towns were considered prime targets. In regard to foreign missions, Eliot had commented after the first Unitarian Missionary Conference in 1913, "The prevailing opinion is that foreign missionaries are more or less an impertinence."[2] The association was not committed to mission work in Jamaica, and they gave Brown support only because they saw his work as a humanitarian effort and felt it their social responsibility to help improve the life of blacks.

At the core of the denomination's response was an attitude of elitism and racism. Samuel Eliot and Louis Cornish saw themselves as the benefactors of this downtrodden race. These men may have accepted that the souls of all people were equal before God and their rights equal before the law, but the educated, upper-class white man's moral and intellectual superiority was unquestioned. They extended themselves to Brown as the result of a paternalistic reflex, but did not treat him like an equal. The deep resentment that Cornish later felt toward Brown arose out of his perception of Brown as an ungrateful child. Cornish felt wronged by this Jamaican who confronted his racist attitudes.

By the end of Cornish's administration in 1937, the attitudes of the officials of the American Unitarian Association had changed; they were now interested in making inroads into the black community. Brown began receiving support, but the hopes of Dale DeWitt, A. Powell Davies, and others were more than could be satisfied. A number of black ministers passed by, but there were no places to settle them. White churches were out of the question, and there was little money to finance a project in the black community. As the racial consciousness of the Unitarian ministry continued to evolve, ministers became more active in race relations. A few churches became integrated. By the time Unitarians began looking seriously at the black community, Brown was an old man. To him, they had given too little, too late. His time had passed. In Chicago, McGee, never knowing the details of Brown's courageous struggle, received denominational support as a matter of course. Beyond this, the denomination was at a loss as to how to initiate a relevant program.

The association's board of directors established and mandated the Commission on Unitarian Intergroup Relations in 1952 and accepted its report in 1954. The report was thorough and searching. The commission sent questionnaires to all Unitarian churches and received responses from 170, or about one third of them. Of these churches fifty-two had black voting members, and of this group thirteen had five or more black members.[3] Two of these churches were the Harlem Unitarian Church and the Free Religious Fellowship.

In defining the problem, the commission wrote:

In all too many of the communications we have received, there is clear evidence that Unitarians are not brought to a test of their interracial idealism because many Unitarian churches cater to social classes which contain few or no Negroes. They are located often in neighborhoods or communities from which Negroes are generally excluded. Some churches, located in a neighborhood whose character has changed, face the decision whether to stay or to move out to a more stable suburb.

The commission had found that many of the churches that had no blacks in their community (forty-five) felt the issue was not relevant for them. The commission also cautioned those who thought they knew about blacks because blacks worked for them that people in an employer-employee relationship seldom reach "a degree of understanding of each as unique personalities." The commission found generally that the two communities were so isolated from one another that it was difficult to see how meaningful relationships could be built without a conscious effort. But the opinion of a majority of the churches surveyed was that "there should be no special program for attracting nonwhites . . . Unitarianism, not interracial relations, was their objective." Only twenty-four of the churches had taken specific action to reach out to the black community. Some had advertised in black newspapers, but the most successful were those visibly active in race relations in their communities. Knowing that this was the direction in which less-active churches needed to move and yet faced with the reality of congregational autonomy, the commission determined that the AUA administration must take the moral initiative. They recognized the need to exert leadership, but also the fact that "people, not organization, will have to do the job."

After considering the denomination as a whole, the commission found the association was making significant contributions to race relations through its religious education curriculum, the *Christian Register*, Beacon Press, and the Harlem Service Camp of the Unitarian Service Committee. The commission formed its opinion into specific recommendations. They asserted that an " 'Open Door' policy is not truly one unless all perceive it to be so." Churches that did not want to make a special effort were settling for the status quo. (The Evening Alliance of the First Unitarian Church of Chicago had realized this six years earlier.) The commission proposed that statements declaring the church's openness to all people should be made at the congregational, district, and denominational levels; that committees for study and action should be formed, and that churches should be ready to accept black ministers and regional organizations be ready to recommend them. The commission also recommended that the next general conference be held at Fisk University following the annual Fisk race relations conference so that Unitarians might conveniently attend both and that a pilot project with an interracial ministry be created in the Durham–Raleigh–Chapel Hill area of North Carolina.

The report concluded:

One can draw no other conclusion from the studies of this Commission than that the majority of our churches have ignored the human relations aspect of religion. While paying lip service to the religious ideals of brotherhood, they have sanctioned, often simply in indifference, a pattern of social organization which dooms men to a life in which full dignity and creative growth are virtually impossible. This is a particularly disturbing indictment of a church committed to freedom on all its various aspects. Almost no one will admit he denies the concept of equality of all men even though in practice he may deny it with every breath. We are tragically bound by an emotional strait-jacket from which escape is possible only through the efforts of men and women of unusual courage, humility, and integrity who have the energy and vision to take the lead in demonstrating their strong beliefs in freedom and a new way of life. Such men and women are appearing in increasing numbers throughout our land. Unitarianism has a rightful place of leadership in this awakening; it can claim it boldly and courageously facing up to the social realities of the time.

"The Church that is to lead this century will not be a church creeping on all fours, mewling and whining, its face turned down, its eyes turned back . . . it will try things by reason and conscience, aim to surpass the old heroes; and, using the present age, will lead public opinion, not follow it."

This prophecy of "The Coming Church," by Theodore Parker, reaches out to us from the past to emphasize obligations necessary for any church which would lead its community.

. . . It is not enough to help the Negro, it is not enough to provide for him; it is the responsibility of the local church to welcome him, to respect him, to respect his dignity, and to treat him as an equal.

. . . The call is for it to turn its face upward, its eyes forward, to accept the challenge and to move unflinchingly toward the development of a religious movement in which all may be participants without thought of racial or national origin. When that shall have been fully accomplished the obligations of the liberal faith shall have been fulfilled and the democratic spirit will have been given complete expression in the vital affairs of men.[4]

The report is testimony to how much the American Unitarian Association had changed during the half century that

Ethelred Brown had been associated with it. At last the association had taken official stock of the situation, understood its dynamics, and set specific goals. But despite their good intentions, the commission's proposals were never implemented. The general conference did not meet at Fisk; the pilot project in North Carolina was never established; two years after the release of the report the Congregational Unitarian Church of Flint, Michigan, refused to settle Lewis McGee; and not until 1961, when McGee was called to the Chico Unitarian Fellowship in Bayside, California, did a black man become the senior minister of a white Unitarian church. Progress was slow.

The Unitarian church was not integrated because it chose not to be. The church housed ordinary people with grand ideas about themselves, and the denomination was run by men who were no different. Often their understanding was limited and their vision too weak to see beyond the status quo or beyond the narrow appeal of the Unitarian church. They were captives of the American caste system. Paternalistic in their racism, Unitarian leaders at the beginning of the twentieth century did not respect the black man. Slowly, over a period of decades, some Unitarians began to see their way out of this, but it was still difficult to break the patterns of segregation that were demographically and socially perpetuated. Even for those who wanted to change, serious risks and major efforts were required.

The racist attitudes of Unitarian officials explain, in part, why efforts to introduce Unitarianism to the black community failed. In the prime of life, Brown had to divert his energies to struggling for economic survival and fighting with the American Unitarian Association, but when he finally gained official support in his later years, he had no greater success in attracting new members to his church. This suggests that more than racism prevented the Unitarian denomination from stirring the black community. The door to Unitarianism may have been barely open to blacks, but this alone cannot explain why the Unitarian message failed to attract blacks. This brings us to our second question: Why did the black community respond to Unitarianism as it did, even when the message was proclaimed by men like Brown and McGee? In the lives of these two individuals Unitarianism was a lived faith, and that faith was refracted by the prism of black experience. In Brown's and McGee's lives we find images that reveal in what ways Unitarianism was relevant to the black experience and how it responded to the needs of the black community.

Central to Brown's decision to enter the ministry was the crisis he faced when he lost his position as a clerk in the treasury in Jamaica. The idea of ministry, which had lain dormant for a time, was reawakened. His parents had predicted it; he had played at it in his youth; and the question had reemerged when his brother had sailed to Africa as a missionary and when Brown was a lay leader in a Methodist church. In the days of crisis, of dishonor, of loss, of not knowing what to do next, Brown turned to the ministry. This could have been an act of penance, for he concluded that God's will had been calling him to the ministry and the loss of his job was the price he paid for resisting. After deciding to become a minister, he then had to decide which faith he would serve. He chose Unitarianism, and he held adamantly to this choice throughout his life. He never wavered again.

A second crisis came with the final withdrawal of American Unitarian Association support from the Jamaican mission. Brown's heated correspondence accomplished nothing; abandoned and humiliated by the American Unitarian Association, he carried on alone. He sustained his family by working as a junior master and received some small aid from the English Alliance of Unitarian Women. Finally, personal financial disaster threatened, and he was unable to continue his ministry. This crisis led to his departure for New York. He sailed with one thought in his mind—to start a Unitarian church in Harlem. Once again in crisis, Brown's foremost commitment was to the Unitarian ministry. It demanded great sacrifices from him and held his loyalty.

A third crisis, or more accurately a series of crises, enveloped him at the end of his employment by the Socialist party. His primary commitment was to the church, and he could not bring himself to go back to menial labor that interfered with his ministry. Jobless, he began soliciting for the Harlem church from Unitarian ministers. He was warned that his name would be removed from the ministerial rolls if he continued. He ceased for a time, but was under incredible pressure: His wife was mentally ill; his eldest son committed suicide; and another son, an alcoholic, was institutionalized. Caught in this desperate situation, Brown once again solicited aid from his colleagues, and this time he was removed from fellowship. It took Brown five years to be reinstated, but he fought that battle with the same determination with which he challenged anything that stood between him and his ministry.

Brown was loyal to the Unitarian ministry because, from his initial decision in 1907 until his death in 1956, it was the dominant force in his life. He saw his relationship to the ministry as a marriage, and his fidelity never waned. He was ultimately committed to the role of the minister. He turned to it in every moment of crisis, and it gave his life structure, context, and goals. But this role of minister is not a central element in the Unitarian faith; it was only the receptacle of Brown's faith. His faith in and need to fill the ministerial role above all else explain the sudden end of the Harlem Unitarian Church after Brown's death. The church had little life apart from him, for it was Brown who held it together, rather than the members' commitment to liberal religion. Those who were committed went to other Unitarian churches. By contrast, McGee focused on the community, and he assisted church members in building a community that managed to survive. Many of the commitments he nurtured early in the life of the Free Religious Fellowship have endured. McGee clearly had a different relationship to his ministry: He held it in perspective, sacrificing neither himself nor his family for the cause of liberal religion.

Brown saw himself as a minister, but this is not the image I choose to isolate in order to define his life and work. An image is a metaphor that traditionally embodies the content of faith. The ministerial role gave structure and direction to Brown's life, but was subsumed in his perception of himself as a "suffering servant." That is, ministry provided the framework, but his real sense of himself was his identity as the "suffering servant." Brown did not use this expression himself, but the attitude behind this image permeates his letters and sermons and the image is the dominant one of his life. "Of all I suffered in those days I dare not write," he said referring to his struggles after taking up the Unitarian cause in Jamaica.[5] In later years he recalled that when the American Unitarian Association withdrew its support, he "struggled on against great odds facing public disgrace and ruin."[6] He regularly wrote Boston to tell them how much he had suffered for the cause. Nowhere does he evoke this image more powerfully than in the hymn he sent to the directors of the association: "The price I pay, the price I pay, the price I pay—the cross I bear."[7] In a sermon entitled "My Faith—Then and Now," Brown's identification with Jesus was clearly articulated:

> As the years have rolled on Jesus has become more and more my ideal and my inspiration. In the hours of bitterness when I have been hurt—when I would hate those who have hindered me and who have even tried to rob me of my good name—I have turned my eyes to the cross of the crucified Nazarene, and I have looked and heard his immortal prayer: "Father forgive them, for they know not what they do," and I have forgiven. In the crises when the tempter pointed to me the apparently easier way, but the way which lay not in the path of duty but led to the road of cowardly compromise, I have seen Jesus in the Garden of Gethsemane fighting a similar battle, and steadfastly walked to Jerusalem, to Calvary and to his cross, and I was strengthened to lose, if for awhile I must lose, but to be true. Thus has Jesus come to be for me the Master of the Spirit.[8]

Brown knew himself to be a disciple of Jesus, a suffering servant, a martyr for the liberal cause who bore Unitarianism

into what he saw as the religiously backward and super-
stitious black community. In doing this he suffered, but
his task gave the struggle meaning. For it was a self-initi-
ated suffering that came from following the demands of
his conscience, a suffering that came as the price of remaining true to his convictions. The reward was the sense
of self-worth and dignity he found in holding fast to what
he knew to be true. The theme of suffering links Brown to
the black religious tradition, where the concept of suffering is central to the teachings on faith and redemption.
Within the black religious tradition, suffering is compen-
sated for by the dignity that comes from knowing the one
who suffers is chosen by God. And the reward for suffering
is found in one's connection with God. This connection,
the same one that sustained the slave on a day-to-day basis,
was ultimately directed toward the afterlife.

Brown's attitude does not belong entirely to the black
tradition. Unitarians believe that people suffer for their
actions or beliefs, although that suffering is not central to
faith. From the middle-class perspective, suffering is viewed
as a result of one's private actions, not as an inevitable
experience in this world. Suffering, for blacks, was a corporate and universal given. For Unitarians, suffering was an
isolated, individual burden that was taken on voluntarily.
For the Unitarian, the dignity of suffering was found, not
in one's relationship to God, but in one's relationship to
oneself, the result of one's commitment to personal values
or conscience. In addition, Unitarians do not emphasize
the afterlife, and consequently, the traditional black reward
for suffering is denied.

Brown had to reconcile the belief of the disinherited in
the almost consuming presence of suffering with the middle-

class concept of individual suffering. For the disinherited, suffering was inherent in reality. It was part of existence, and relief came through grace. For the middle-class white, suffering was a personal choice related to one's ideals.

Brown understood suffering as a central part of his existence. Even as a child, his favorite hymn had been "Oh Paradise, T'is Weary Waiting Here." He recalled, "I sang it often, and as I sang my face was bathed in tears."[9] Brown attempted to reach the black community through this common belief in suffering, but Brown's concept of suffering was too clearly Unitarian. In his sermon "The Price We Pay," his message was this:

> Choose, my friends, but know in choosing, that you shall be paid for what you have done . . . to obtain the object of your choice you must always pay the price. Choose, then, my brethren, choose. What will you have? Pay the price and take it.

Suffering was here related to individual choice, as a voluntary state of existence and as a personal burden. The black disinherited, under the burden of American life, could not make sense of this message. Only as blacks moved into the middle class could they understand Brown's message. Moreover, once they achieved middle-class status, the religious centrality of suffering diminished. Remarkably, Brown's experience of suffering came out of both traditions. By contrast, for McGee, who portrayed the more typical middle-class liberal response, suffering was no longer central.

Brown and McGee shared more in the area of their idealism and ideals. Brown's idealism filled his writing, and his ideals drew the "suffering servant" ever onward. His initial high hopes for the Jamaican mission supported him when it became transparently clear that the denomination would eventually abandon him. Again and again, Brown had expectations and dreams that seemed to ignore reality and often led to irresponsible action. Indeed, he built failure into his mission by consistently taking on too much. When Brown preached "that men who visualize better days and believed that visions may become true were really 'practical,'" he was articulating a conviction by which he lived.[10] But visions may also be held for self-defense, for without them Brown would have been overwhelmed by his life's legacy of despair.

By contrast, McGee's idealism was not the result of a desperate need to leave today's pain for tomorrow's dreams. McGee had a desire to see Unitarianism proclaimed to the black community and he was committed to the ministry, but it was not the center of his life. Methodically, thoughtfully, cautiously he approached his endeavor, understanding his limits. His idealism did not serve to sustain an illusion, but rather guided him to an attainable goal.

In spite of their different approaches, Brown and McGee nevertheless shared the single ideal of establishing Unitarianism in the black community and nurtured an idealism that helped them to achieve their individual goals. In pursuing their ideal both were clearly rooted in the belief in human perfectibility and progress and in the hope for social justice that are the recurrent proclamations of liberal religion.

Brown's allegiance to the ministerial role and his idealism are subsumed within the dynamics of the image of the "suffering servant," but this image is not a dominant one in the Unitarian tradition. Its centrality is only particular to Brown's message. To move beyond Brown's idiosyncrasies to the distinctive Unitarian elements of the message he brought to Harlem, we must consider the institutional life of the Harlem church. The Harlem Unitarian Church was called a temple and a forum. These words convey the church's self-understanding and define a dual purpose that was never synthesized but was manifest as institutional schizophrenia. Was their primary function worship or intellectual dialogue? They were not sure. The church won its acclaim primarily through its role as a forum. The quality of the speakers and discussions drew people—largely young men—who were hungry for intellectual stimulation.

Brown valued intellectual freedom highly, and this was dramatically illustrated when he was attacked after conducting a worship service. On that evening after speaking in favor of the deportation of Marcus Garvey, he had tried to conduct an orderly discussion, but he was a Unitarian. He could not manage people for whom speaking was merely a weapon. He persisted in his efforts to bring the meeting to order, but after failing to stimulate an intelligent and orderly discussion, he ended the service and was assaulted as he left the room. The church underwent a similar experience when meetings were invaded by communists, who held ideology above the free exchange of ideas. To rid the church of such people, Brown had to switch to a strict worship format. He did this to protect what was central to the religious community—intellectual inquiry and dialogue. For Brown and the Harlem Unitarian Church, intellectual freedom was not the handmaiden of politics; the former reigned supreme.

The question facing the Harlem church concerned, not the importance of "seeking the truth in freedom," but the context within which that search should occur. The style of worship vacillated between the secular and the religious. This issue did not arise for the Free Religious Fellowship. McGee's content was intellectually stimulating and included the political element, but there was no confusion of purpose. Politics did not overpower the experience of worship.

In both churches, political freedom was important. The great difference between the two was that Brown was more outspoken in the community. A political radical and an orator of some eloquence, Brown attracted people who were not as interested in free religion as they were in radical politics and other specifically secular concerns.

Both churches attracted socialists and other political activists; in both, sermons addressed pressing social issues. Intellectual freedom and political freedom were closely aligned. This was also true of Jeffrey Campbell's ministry, and similar concerns were evident among the black Universalists in Suffolk and Norfolk, Virginia, who as part of their mission at first established schools and later the Jordan Neighborhood House. It is clear that there is a strong link for blacks involved in liberal religion between intellectual concerns and social or political concerns. These areas of interest seem to work in tandem, reinforcing one another. What only the most conscientious and radical of white Unitarian ministers had done all these ministers, Brown, McGee, Campbell, and the Jordans, had done naturally. Theirs was the legacy of blackness. With segregation the norm and discrimination always present, blacks knew life was not simply a matter of individual freedom, and black Unitarian ministers knew they had to strive after freedom for all blacks in America. Theirs was a broad understanding of freedom that encompassed involvement in the economic mainstream and political representation. Political freedom was more tangible for blacks because it could never be taken for granted. The outspoken Ethelred Brown felt deeply about all injustice, and saw the role of the church as the challenger of inequities. Brown was saying this at a time when most black churches focused on other-worldly concerns, and he railed at the irresponsibility of the orthodox black ministers.

The question of political freedom had rarely been directly addressed by most black churches. They regarded the spiritual as their realm. Brown fought against this attitude, which he associated with emotionalism, superstition, and escapism. Brown hoped to liberate the minds of blacks from the smothering embrace of orthodox Christianity. McGee also reacted negatively to the emotional, other-worldly quality of traditional black religion. In their own churches, they both presented spirituality as a reverent contemplative state. They offered no place for the ecstatic experience.

The absence of ecstatic experience in the religious lives of Brown and McGee is significant. According to Cecil Cone, ecstatic experience is the essence of black faith. This experience marks the encounter with God that allows one to place entire trust in Him and achieve dignity as one of His children. Brown's and McGee's conversions, if we can call them that, to Unitarianism were of a different nature. As inquisitive children and then as educated adults, they had begun to doubt orthodox dogma and eventually their consciences forced on them a choice between their traditions and what they knew to be true. Thus for them, the basic religious experience was not an ecstatic encounter with God but rather an act of individual will, an act of conscience. Even for Brown, who at one time attributed to God his decision to enter the ministry, the mailing of that fateful letter to "any Unitarian Minister in New York City" was the act of a man tormented by his conscience.[11] This explains the lack of spiritual focus in the worship of their religious communities, for it was not the primary element in their commitment to Unitarianism.

Brown and McGee were Unitarian in outlook, and freedom was seen in a Unitarian light in their churches. Intellectual freedom was primary. Political freedom was also valued highly and closely aligned with intellectual freedom. This was perhaps the most vital aspect of these two communities. The connection between political and intellectual freedom was felt, not because the preacher castigated them, as is the case in some white churches, but because they knew oppression of the mind and body. Black Unitarians were still striving for both freedoms. Spiritual freedom, which was associated with orthodoxy and was not part of the conversion experience to Unitarianism, was contemplative not ecstatic.

Brown and McGee had moved rapidly away from black religion. Brown, a theist who believed God was spirit and Jesus a moral exemplar, emphasized people's responsibility for themselves and the world. He railed at the black church that transferred people's "interest from here and now to existence in some other world" and "destroys personal responsibility." He believed that salvation came through "character and service" and that "every man must work out his own salvation."[12] McGee, a humanist, was theologically the more radical of the two. But, like Brown, he was unequivocal in insisting that "we choose our destiny."[13]

Yet even with these solidly middle-class beliefs, Brown

and McGee conform to a limited degree with H. Richard
Niebuhr's description of the disinherited. Like the middle-
class religionists, the black Unitarians' messages emphasized individualistic tendencies in which striving super-
sedes grace as the means of salvation. In Unitarian fashion
they relied upon ideas and concepts, as is evident in the
paucity of images that have emerged from their writings
and their lives. But unlike the middle-class churches and
more like the churches of the disinherited, these black
Unitarians maintained a sense of corporate redemption.
Although the burden of action rested upon the individual,
as Unitariansim holds, not God, the awaited result was still
the liberation of the oppressed, a belief distinctly associated
with black religion. Worldly salvation would come as an
event that freed the black community from economic oppression and discrimination. In addition, as we have seen,
the members of the Harlem Unitarian Church and the
Free Religious Fellowship had strong social consciences,
and this too is a quality of black religion. Gayraud Wilmore
asserts that this feature of social concern generates the
"ambivalence about religious and secular objectives [that]
has been a characteristic of black religion in America."[14]
In America the social disparity between whites and blacks
is so obvious and the injustice so inescapable that secular
objectives, primarily the demand for a just society, is always an urgent one. So regardless of whether a religion was
spiritually or intellectually oriented, ambivalence arises as
the political dimension presses to the fore, sometimes overwhelming the other important aspects of faith.

Interestingly, when political freedom emerged during
the civil rights era as a religious quest and value, the black
church, Unitarianism, and other white denominations were

able to form an alliance. Martin Luther King, Jr., was
able to mesh the elements of spirituality and political and
intellectual freedom with biblical and democratic traditions. For a time this gave Unitarians, black and white,
shared goals and a corporate identity. And it was during
this time that liberal churches attracted larger numbers of
blacks than ever before. Part of this influx was due to the
rising economic status of the black American, but part was
a response to a liberal message that for a time proclaimed
the political aspect of freedom.

Who were the black people who became Unitarians?
They were generally educated, often Methodist, as were
Brown and McGee, and usually middle class. Brown and
McGee knew exactly who their message appealed to: the
educated, the cultured, and the prosperous. These were the
people who had begun to question black religion and
whose interests had expanded beyond the black community. The report of the Commission on Unitarian Intergroup Relations identified the same group of people as
prospective Unitarians:

> The Commission believes that there is a considerable
> reservoir of non-white people for Unitarianism.
> . . . Primary among these . . . are college graduates
> who can no longer reconcile their advanced scientific
> knowledge with teachings common to the fundamen-
> talist tradition. Then there have been others, just
> plain people, not college graduates or people with
> formal education, who raise questions about the
> concern of God and Jesus for their plight as Negroes
> in America. They find difficulty in reconciling
> their long continuing oppression in our Christian
> community with their expectation that Jesus would

be pleading their cause at the throne of grace, bringing them relief and solace. To many Negroes the highly emotional content of worship services is objectionable and often embarrassing. Yet because of their early religious training, many would prefer to have some church connection. They stand in a dilemma.

Yet even as this commission identified prospective Unitarians, the fact remains that few blacks responded to Brown and McGee. There is no simple explanation for this. One contributing factor is the great disparity between the perspectives of the disinherited black and the middle-class Unitarian. Another factor the commission touched on:

> Some Negroes are active in churches for personal business reasons but secretly do not subscribe to the religion they profess. Others go to church simply because relatives and friends expect it of them. Many are silent about their beliefs, fearing that the mass pressure of friends and relatives will brand them with "heresy."[15]

What the commission is alluding to here is the pressure the black community puts on its members. To become a Unitarian one had to forsake the community by stepping outside its accepted set of beliefs. This was a serious risk for blacks, because in doing this they challenged the community they depended upon for support. We saw this in the disfavor Brown's pronouncement of Unitarian beliefs met in Montego Bay. (Brown's experience is perhaps more comparable to an immigrant's leaving the faith of the old country than to the average suburbanite's commitment to a Unitarian church.) It is not surprising, then, that black Unitarian churches arose in America's two largest metropolises, where the communal bonds were looser.

Joining a church outside the traditional black community was a risk that only a few were able to take. They were among the few for whom wider vistas had already opened, the few who were already or were in the process of becoming middle class. Financially secure, they depended less upon a community church. They had already begun to see beyond the community and therefore could step out of it. They had broader social, political, and cultural commitments and wanted a church that could support these. They did not want or need the experience of a tightknit community, for they had just escaped this narrow world. The tentativeness of people's commitment to the Free Religious Fellowship and the Harlem Unitarian Church was characteristic of these new churches, for these involved black people, many of them young men, who had no desire to be locked into Unitarianism when they were just discovering a larger world.

The group we have been discussing was a small one, and their experience and needs different from the majority, who generally supported the community church. When Richard Allen first established the African Methodist Episcopal church in 1794, he did so with the early assistance of Benjamin Rush, who understood that this was an important act of self-assertion. In the black church the Afro-American was his own person who could run his own affairs and stand with dignity. The church's functions were broad: Its members cared for the sick, helped the poor, provided day care services for children, and prepared the dead for burial; they were social welfare agencies and more. They had choirs, basketball teams, and literary clubs. For many people the black church was the center of the community.

Beyond the day to day lie the years upon years that the black church had spent with the Afro-American in slavery and hard times. The Bible and the spirituals of black religion were imbibed with mother's milk. Blacks needed a way of explaining their suffering and maintaining their hope, and the church answered their call. They needed a place to rejoice and a place to weep, and the church was there. They needed a companion and Jesus came. Much of their lives was out of control, and they had learned, in the recognition of their powerlessness, to depend on something outside themselves. And that was God. It was not easy to break away from the black church and from a loyalty that had been forged over centuries. Harry I. Jones, a founding member of the Free Religious Fellowship, returned to orthodoxy late in his life. The pull was strong.

The church had evolved in response to the needs of black people. It had responded to the black call for help. Yet as people broke into the larger culture and experienced aspects of American life that had earlier been denied them, the black church began to lose some of its relevance. As black people gained more control over their lives and experienced a dignity won through personal achievements seemingly independent of God, they could begin to move away from mother church.

Brown and McGee could not help reacting to the orthodoxy they were raised with and left as adults. They diminished God's role and instead of relating Unitarianism to the full black experience—including spirituality—disassociated themselves from black emotionalism and overidentified with Unitarian intellectualism. To move as rapidly as they did from a spiritually centered religion to an intellectually centered one was too great a leap for all but a few.

Howard Thurman's experience reinforces the conclusion that Brown and McGee lost a significant element of the black community in their radical move. When Thurman was called to the Church for the Fellowship of All Peoples in 1944, the conditions were more advantageous than they had been for Brown and McGee when they began. But beyond the good circumstances, whose significance we should not underestimate, there were two important elements. First, Thurman combined intellectual freedom with spiritual freedom. Thurman was both a highly educated and a profoundly spiritual man; he was a mystic. From an inner strength first nurtured by the God of black religion he had moved outward to establish a religious community whose parameters embraced the religions of the world. He did not reject what was integral to the black religious experience that had sustained him, and blacks and whites alike could therefore come to him without rejecting their own religious heritage. Brown and McGee were rebellious in their transition to a liberal position; Thurman was gradual. Thurman's church was nondenominational and this allowed him more freedom to adapt liberal theology to a black perspective. Yet if Thurman synthesized the intellectual and spiritual, he approached the political in a circuitous manner. His church community thrived in part because he did not address controversial and disruptive issues head on, as Brown had. For Thurman, the church was always a worshiping community first, and never a forum. He approached basic social change by building a religious fellowship, a "beachhead" that cut across all racial and cultural barriers. The church's role was to inspire its members through worship and fellowship to take "personal responsibilities for social change." Thurman explained his understanding in this way: "It was my conviction and determination that the church would be a resource for activists—a mission fundamentally perceived. To me it was important that individuals who were in the thick of the struggle for social change would be able to find renewal and fresh courage in the spiritual resources of the church. There must be provided a place, a moment, when a person could declare, 'I choose!'"[16] Second, Thurman, whom the black historian Lerone Bennett described as a "twentieth-century holy man," had charisma, a personal magnetism that defies analysis but can mean everything when it comes to assuming leadership of a group of people.

One denominational officer was heard to remark that if Eugene Sparrow was only another "Howard Thurman," they would have no problem placing him.[17] This is sadly an accurate appraisal. The barriers of race were so overwhelming that only someone with the spiritual depth and national stature of a Howard Thurman could have succeeded. It is only fair to assert that Ethelred Brown would have made a fine minister in less-demanding times, and indeed he was successful in other areas of his public life. Lewis McGee, similarly, had many successful pastorates. But the task they undertook to introduce Unitarianism into the black community was great, the demands large, and the time not quite right. Brown's life was tragic. His ministerial hubris, in combination with his high idealism, all but destroyed his family. Moreover, he was buffeted by the racial and political divisions within the black community and by the effects of war and the Depression. We cannot really know how much of his failure was simply due to the momentum of history, to Eliot's and Cornish's bigotry, and to Brown's own actions. McGee came to Unitarianism a mature man; he was not dynamic but rather methodical and studious on the one hand and possessed by a wanderlust on the other. A warm and personable, if undemonstrative, man, he does not seem a likely candidate for enlivening a movement. The reality was that both of these men took on enormous tasks, tasks that we with the advantage of hindsight can say were beyond their personal resources given a denomination that never made the Unitarian mission into the black community a priority.

The Commission on Unitarian Intergroup Relations (l. to r.): Dr. Howard Thurman, Albert D'Orlando, Dr. Errold D. Collymore, Dr. Alfred McClung Lee (chair), Raymond M. Wheeler, Dr. Frederick May Eliot, Charles N. Mason, Jr., Arthur Foote. Lillian Smith, a member of the commission, was not present for this picture. (1954).

Chapter Five

Integration Where It Counts

> This church is dedicated to the proposition that beneath all our diversity, behind all our differences, there is a unity which makes us one and binds us forever together in spite of time and death and the space between the stars.
> DAVID E. BUMBAUGH, JR.

The experiences of Ethelred Brown and Lewis McGee reinforce the conclusion that Unitarianism is a class-bound religion. These men were Unitarian in their beliefs, attitudes, and messages, and they understandably attracted others of the same mold. But Brown and McGee deviated from Unitarian norms in one significant way: For both of them political freedom was closely related to intellectual freedom. Other than this one exception, they had limited success in integrating the significant elements of black religion with Unitarianism. Such a synthesis may have had broader appeal in the black community, but we have little idea what this synthesis might have looked like. The question inherent in the lives of Brown and McGee remains: How can the liberal faith and black religion enrich one another?

To answer this question, we must consider not only blacks but also other groups who feel a burden in their lives. In this book traditional black religion in the United States has been considered a religion of the disinherited, of those whose central experience in life is oppression and powerlessness. The working class has known a similar experience, but its master is industry. In the factory workers sell their labor, but do not own what their time produces. Their alienation from the product they make and the lack of control over the working environment seems to engender a sense of fatalism if not powerlessness. Until now I have emphasized racial segregation, but class segregation is just as pervasive, if not more so. Indeed, the main barrier facing those who would enter the liberal religious community is class. This point is convincingly argued by Dan Dale and Eric Haugan in "Class and Conflict: The Declining Influence of Religion in Unitarian Universalism."[1] Liberal churches welcome blacks and others who have assimilated middle-class values.

We have discussed the conditions in black life that shaped black religion, and why Unitarianism did not address these conditions, but we have not examined the liberal church from the black perspective. To help us do so, I will first discuss Robert Coles's essay "Work and Self-Respect," which analyzes the intellectual community from the working-class perspective, because the workers' criticisms of the intellectual community are analogous to those blacks make of Unitarianism.

The major criticism made by the working class of the intellectual community is its propensity to indulge in self-scrutiny. Coles points out that members of the working class have "an aversion to it." The reason for this negative appraisal of self-scrutiny is twofold. First, the ordinary person sees it as a "matter of time and money. Who, they wonder, has the luxury of hours to spend talking about himself or herself, and his or her ideas—and for pay?" The working class certainly does not. Second, workers ask, Where does all this thinking lead? They say, "What can I do? What can anyone do? . . . Nothing, I'll tell you. That's what you learn in life." These two judgments leveled at the intellectual community reveal the basic tension in the working-class ethos between realism and fatalism that shapes workers' attitudes toward the intellectual community.

The first response to self-scrutiny (aversion) is an example of working-class realism. Realists recognize "the fact of life" that they have to work in order to provide for their families. They say, "I don't have time to sit around and think about myself." They do not have time for the luxury of self-examination. Their attitude is, "This is the situation we have to deal with. Let us get on with it and do the best we can." In such situations contemplation is only valuable when it leads quickly to action. From this perspective, thought without action is sterile. Unrealistic goals—the idle dreams that grow in self-scrutiny—are dangerous because they demoralize people. They must be avoided when one's self-respect turns on one's ability to face certain harsh realities.

Thus, the second query, "What's the use?" is a fatalistic one because the worker has a sense that life should be better, yet is quite unwilling to look at that feeling and is at a loss as to what to do about it. When this inchoate feeling of hope does emerge, the worker's fatalism, which is taken to be realism, suppresses the hope again. The worker exclaims, "You don't ask *why* in this life." To contemplate the whys and wherefores of circumstance would be painful, especially if those reflections did not lead to concrete change. They would only serve to affirm a sense of power-lessness and subsequent unworthiness. The worker there-fore curtails self-scrutiny because of his or her inability to bring personal hopes for a better world to fruition. If the worker held on to these hopes in the face of a feeling of powerlessness, the disillusionment might well destroy the redemptive character of work. If the ultimate goal of a better world is unattainable, the immediate goals of work and family—these are in fact the primary sources of mean-ing and values—become ephemeral.

The dichotomy between realism and fatalism in the working-class ethos indicates why so few members of the working class are Unitarian Universalists. As realists they have no faith in the endless self-scrutiny in which Unitar-ian Universalists indulge. Intellectual stimulation without tangible results does not attract them, although the purg-ing effect of emotional religion and other-worldly rewards may. Members of the working class are pragmatic realists who demand that thought lead to action. For the fatalistic part of the worker's character, the questions raised in some religious liberal churches are just too painful. "The trouble with going to church—I told the priest once—is that you get to thinking, and thinking and thinking afterwards. But what can you do? Nothing . . ."[2]

From the working-class perspective, intellectuals talk about things they can do nothing about, and do nothing about the things they talk about. This criticism rings true. It points to a problem raised in the first chapter: the Uni-tarian tendency to abuse intellectual freedom by becoming esoteric in one's thinking. This tendency can be corrected by learning from the experience of black religion, which tries to unite thought and action to improve the lives of its members.

Liberal religion needs working-class realism. Despite the black church's reputation for other-worldliness, it has met the needs of the present. Child care, food and shelter, funerary matters, the cause of civil rights, and voter registration are all concerns to which the black church has responded. It was in their political concerns that Brown, McGee, and the members of their churches dovetailed with black religion. The situation of blacks in America has always served to make political freedom a pressing issue and this is where Brown and McGee endeavored to unite the two traditions. But we have seen that the balance between the political and the religious in Brown's Unitarianism was precarious. This can be traced to the ever-present dilemma over the church's role in society, for Brown saw social concern as integral to the religious community.

However, the primary function of the church is as a "temple," not as a "forum." Whatever transpires needs to happen in the context of a worshiping community. It is there that people bear witness to and celebrate their roots in Universal life. It is in this time and space set apart that people recognize an intimacy with the world that pervades life at all times. Here the elements of spirituality in religion draw us beyond the intellect to the felt connection with a personal God. It was in this relationship that the slave found dignity, for it cut across all distinctions and touched one's essential humanness. Dignity, which cannot be impinged upon by slavery, does not take class, race, or achievement into consideration. As a Unitarian Universalist who has not known a saving experience, I wonder at Cecil Cone's assertion that this relationship is marked by an ecstatic event, but I do not question that this experience of connectedness is the essential spiritual element in religion. This connection and consequent human dignity are inherent in life, and this inherent dignity answers two middle-class problems. First, it bestows forgiveness on the vulnerable individual who inevitably fails in an achievement-oriented society. And, second, it destroys the walls of isolation around those who feel that dignity can only rest upon personal achievement.

What does each of us need to know? That we are valued and that our lives have significance. We struggle to acquire the same sense of somebodiness that the slaves desired. But they knew that activity could not achieve this feeling. It had to be a gift. Yet as a gift, it undercuts activity, revealing that the source of value is Being itself. It is this that sustains life. But how does one express loyalty to an intellectually abstract concept like Being itself? This need points to the necessity of a spiritual realm, for it is on this level that one senses or knows the ultimate connectedness of existence. To truly value oneself is to value that which undergirds life. To do this shatters all illusions of isolation. One begins to experience the suffering of others as if it were one's own, and to act to alleviate it.

For the middle class, this process is initiated by a passive act of power. We listen so deeply to the stories of others that we begin to know their pain. To open ourselves to that which we know will be painful is an act of strength. And having done this we can act with a commitment and a conviction that are unlike the noblesse oblige the directors of the American Unitarian Association felt toward Brown, unlike the paternalism that motivated Cornish and Eliot, and unlike the guilt that motivates middle-class liberals today. This conviction is tied to our concepts of ourselves. We are struggling for ourselves, but our self-understanding has broadened. We realize self-interest goes beyond ourselves and our families.

Such a realization has always posed a problem for people like Ethelred Brown who sacrifice themselves and their families for the greater good. These people fall back into a middle-class individualism that stresses their individual responsibilities. Their sense of somebodiness once again attaches itself to their achievements. In reality they cannot feel a sense of worth by themselves because such transformation is an act of community, and each member can only sustain his or her activity to the extent that he or she receives the support of the group. When they find themselves isolated, leaders tend to lose the sense of connectedness that motivated them in the beginning. They continue to work, not for others, but for the cause in which they have invested themselves.

This pitfall not withstanding, Brown remained loyal to his cause because fundamentalist religion and racial discrimination confronted him daily and Unitarianism offered him some scope for challenging these experiences. The immediacy of oppression drove other black Unitarians as well to be active in social reform, and their role in challenging racism has benefited the liberal church as well as the black community. When blacks are members of white denominations and share equally in the life of the community, then racial slurs and discrimination can no longer be shrugged off: They become a personal offense, and overcoming racism takes on an urgency it formerly lacked. To further understanding, the black presence must include the telling of the black story. Moreover, the American story is incomplete without the black story and our national self-understanding is inadequate. The black story is essential if we are to develop an accurate perception of reality to inspire correct action.

The church, as the sustaining institution of a worshiping community, is essential in bringing the elements of spiritual, political, and intellectual freedom into a complementary dynamic. The black church has long housed the spiritual element that Unitarianism needs. It is the experience of spiritual connectedness that sustains a lasting commitment to a just society and places the intellectual and political in perspective. Spirituality provides the motivation, intellectualism provides the tools, and politics is the method. An understanding of the three-dimensionality of freedom, as rooted in the worshiping community, can save us from the esoteric thinking, the misguided politics, and the spiritual vacuity of the Unitarian community.

Clearly Unitarianism has much to gain from black members and black religion, but do the black people and black religion have anything to gain from Unitarianism? And if this question is answered affirmatively, does it not leave the liberal faith with a mission? Must Unitarians and others not commit themselves to overcoming the white middle-class isolation of the liberal faith? Will it not put the universality of the liberal message to the test?

Brown railed against the other-worldliness of black religion. He saw a tendency within the black church to turn its back on this world while in pursuit of the next. There is often an imbalance between the spiritual and political elements in black religion that the Unitarian emphasis on intellectual freedom can help remedy. The fatalism of the disinherited drive them to focus on the other-worldly rather than on justice in this world. In the context of the black church, the spiritual connection to God is emphasized as other-worldly rather than as in and through this world. Power is attributed to God, but it is not recognized that individuals are the primary conduits of His power. God is perceived as all-powerful, and people as powerless. Yet gaining power is one of the central problems in the lives of blacks, workers, and the disinherited. Having power means having the ability to assert control over one's own destiny.

For Unitarians, generally, human participation in God's power is assumed, and for humanists, it is the primary source of power. The basic Unitarian belief that both McGee and Brown proclaimed was "the inherent goodness and rightness of Man," as experienced in "service to humanity." Despite the negative experience of blacks in America, they believed in human perfectibility and progress. The high esteem in which they held humanity and its ability to affect the world was the basis of confidence. Such confidence is essential in overcoming the fatalistic attitude of the oppressed and enabling them to utilize their inherent power—the power the middle class is raised to assume they possess.

Intellectual freedom is the missing element in the spirituality-dominated black church. The free mind does not shrink from questioning the dogmas that sustain the church's fatalism. It can break through the feelings of low self-esteem and the outmoded beliefs that keep people locked into a feeling of helplessness. For it is in reflecting on one's condition that one discovers ways in which to use one's power to bring about a just society. Petitionary prayer cannot do this. Reason is one of the primary methods we have of gaining control of our lives. It helps us go beyond reacting to planning and following our life plans. But when our plans consistently fail for lack of commitment or unrealistic goals, we simply give credence to the belief that talk is cheap. Yet this process, when it leads to results, is affirming and encourages further effort.

Unitarian Universalism at its best models this process. For example, the Unitarian Universalist Association has proven itself the most progressive denomination in integrating women into the ministry, while some black denominations have been among the most recalcitrant in maintaining the ministry as a male domain. The liberal thinker lauds tolerance and reverence for free inquiry and democratic process and sets a scene in which one is forced to look at threatening issues, to discuss them, to be convinced—sometimes after great delays—and finally, if reluctantly, to enter into new realms. Historically Unitarians embraced the heresy that God is one and the Universalists that all are saved. Thus, both continued to leave doctrines behind when truth led on. Today, it is the revelations of feminism to which we respond.

Like all religious traditions, Unitarian Universalism and black religion both proclaim a particular dimension of the truth. Both are significant yet incomplete, and there is adequate ground for mutual enrichment. Each has insights to offer the other. But where do we begin?

There are three courses of action Unitarian Universalists and other liberal religionists may pursue. The first is to continue to talk about and encourage the racial integration of liberal churches. Many profess to want these churches to have a different racial makeup, but the important question is one of motivation. Why do we want to be different?

Despite the Unitarian's roots among the Boston Brahmin, increasingly over the last thirty years there has been a commitment to integration and racial justice. This should imply that Unitarian Universalists prize a multiracial society. But do we? Isn't the stronger impetus a sense of what we ought to be but are not? And this has evoked feelings of dissatisfaction and guilt. It is understandable to be ashamed for Brown's treatment. It is easy to feel guilty about the legacy of fits and starts the Unitarian denomination has left behind. It is hard to unflinchingly accept that we have benefited from society's inequities. But in response, our sense of guilt has led us to pursue integration for the wrong reason: in order to alleviate our conscience. Rather than promising progress, this negative self-image saps us of enthusiasm and robs us of a hopeful vision.

This question of motivation is crucial, and not a simple matter of nuance. To recruit blacks because of our own feelings of moral inadequacy, as our history illustrates, is unreliable and the results are tragic. On the other hand, to see the richness in human diversity and to be excited by its possibility is quite different. Moved by feelings of anticipation, Unitarian Universalists can proclaim a community that is open to all, and to which blacks are invited—as is everyone—not only as individuals but also for the special contribution they make.

A second course of action is to do nothing at all. Given the predominating influence of class in shaping the religious message and the reality of institutional inertia, this is perhaps the most likely scenario. Into our ranks will slowly enter blacks whose experiences and values are not discernibly different from those of other Unitarian Universalists. Nothing dramatic will occur. The persistent and pervasive influence of the mass media and other forces that shape modern consciousness and promote cultural homogeneity along with black economic advances will create conditions under which more blacks will find Unitarian Universalism an attractive option.

As the black middle class expands, several things will happen. The traditional black stereotypes will change. As Stephen Steinberg explains in *The Ethnic Myth: Race, Ethnicity, and Class in America,* "As more blacks achieve middle class respectability, it becomes increasingly difficult for whites to maintain blanket assumptions of racial inferiority."[3] This will mean that blacks entering Unitarian Universalist churches are less likely to be confronted with prejudice and ignorance and thus more likely to remain. In addition, as blacks become more upwardly mobile and involved in the economic mainstream, they will presumably follow the patterns of other ethnic groups, and their kinship ties will weaken. With the economic advance, a lessening of stereotyping, the weakening of kinship networks, and the resulting familiarity with the white world, four obstacles that kept blacks away from liberal religion will be overcome. The experience of both Brown and McGee, in terms of whom they attracted, tends to support this scenario, as does the recent history within the liberal denominations.

A third option for Unitarian Universalists may be to try to change who we are, not by pursuing blacks for the sake of our image, not by waiting until the forces of cultural amalgamation bring us more people like ourselves, but by appreciating who we are and what we have already accomplished, while striving to move beyond our present limits.

We can change because it benefits us. Religious liberals can refuse to be pinned down by the sensibilities of class and instead strive to shape, articulate, and live a religion that takes us beyond the three vaunted principles of freedom, reason, and tolerance toward a more spiritual orientation. In doing so we may meet reality in what is perhaps a profounder and more liberating form. In this new place we may yet discover new faces.

Martin Luther King, Jr., wrote, "Only through inner spiritual transformation do we gain the strength to fight vigorously the evils of the world in a humble and loving spirit." It was individual spirituality that strengthened the slaves, nurtured Martin Luther King, Jr., enlivened black religion, and can perhaps help religious liberalism to further evolve. What is this spirituality and how can Unitarian Universalism introduce it into our religious communities? The Latin word for *spirit* means "breath" or "the breath of God." This spirit comes in many forms and appears in many places, but it always comes as a breath of new life that inspires and revitalizes the human condition. Spirituality allows the individual to span the chasm that divides one from the other. And it reveals to us the eternal truth that all people are one, for the depth of our experience of life is our common bond, our common tongue.

In Unitarianism we can move toward spirituality by moving away from the abstract discursiveness of our sermons toward a profounder use of story. The story itself may be told in many ways: in the sermon, in readings and hymns, through dance. But in each case the objective of our stories must be to engage the whole person. The Bible has endured because the depth and richness of its stories speak to the human condition. Yet this potential rests in many stories. The story of Ethelred Brown's life has seized me. Emotionally, I am angered by both the racism he faced and his neglect of his family. I am saddened by the loss of his son, the fate of his wife, and the end of his Harlem church. And I am in awe of his persistence. One cannot help being touched by the tragic quality of his life. Intellectually, his story raises the issues of racism, internalized oppression, suffering, midlife crisis, commitment, and responsibility. Politically, it points toward the work that has yet to be done. Brown had some success: He did force the American Unitarian Association to look at black America. That limited success was clearly just a beginning. Again, what is important about Brown's story is that the reader is inevitably touched. The element of spirituality is introduced by the identification we feel with Brown. God can never be found in Being itself. Identification with the individual story of Brown links us spiritually to God, who is found in every individual life.

The story is emotionally engaging, politically instructive, intellectually challenging, and spiritually broadening. It connects us to each other despite differences of sex and race, time and space. The story forces us to expand and correct our self-understanding. It is "transsubjective" in that it overcomes subjectivity by forcing us out of our assumed social context and into that of someone else. In the case of Unitarian Universalism, the story of Brown sensitizes whites by providing them with an opportunity to "try on" the black experience. The evocative power of the story breaks through superficial rationalizations to educate and connect us all at a deeper level. Moreover, story is important because of the many levels at which it appeals both to the individual and to the community; story can transcend race and class.

Story puts us into someone else's world. It holds up their struggles and thereby heightens our awareness of our assumptions, the assumptions of the middle class, of the white. In this process one is "liberated into particularity." One's own existence becomes relative and distinctive. This is essentially an event that affirms our individuality. We then move out from the strength of discovery of our somebodiness. That somebodiness is always known in relationship and known best when one can see beyond our differences to the true depth of one's relationship to others.

Although I have emphasized story in the context of the worship service as a means of recognizing spirituality, story is not restricted to this situation. The Spiritual Presence may come at any time because it is not something that one wills. At best, the worship service is a time set apart in which we endeavor to create the conditions that invite a spiritual encounter. The church can never have a monopoly on spirituality—whether it comes in an experience of oneness with nature or a flash of insight in the midst of crisis, whether it be experienced as a serene or an ecstatic event. It comes when it will.

This is the central task of the worshiping community: to invite the Spiritual Presence; to unveil the connectedness of all humanity through the story of life; and thus to reveal this universal truth, which is only discovered amid the particulars of our own lives and the lives of others. Once felt it inspires us to act for justice. The dynamics of intellectual, spiritual, and political freedom occur within the religious community. This loving and supportive association assures us we are not fighting for justice alone, but rather striving as members of a larger community. The religious community is essential, for alone our vision is too narrow to see all that must be seen, and our power too limited to do all that must be done. But together, our vision widens and our strength is renewed.

Chapter Six

"Where There Is No Vision, the People Perish . . ."
(Proverbs 29:18)

Outside, the gray, neo-gothic building that houses Meadville/Lombard Theological School loomed large, dark, silent, and ghostly, except for the light that shone from the window in the basement. On their way home my friends expected to see that light. They assumed that I was studying. What they didn't know was that on some nights I simply buried my head in my arms and wept as the stories unfolded. Sometimes, beneath the bare light bulb of my study carrell, all academic distance was lost. I couldn't believe the stories the documents revealed; I couldn't understand how our religious movement could have done such things. I couldn't even think about it. All I could do was curse and cry. The pain I felt for Ethelred Brown was a pain I would feel for others before finally realizing it was mine, as well.

Egbert Ethelred Brown wasn't the first black minister to proclaim himself a Unitarian and suffer because of it. Our earliest opportunity to spread Unitarianism into the black community came in 1860 when a Rev. Mr. Jackson of New Bedford presented himself to the Autumnal Convention of the American Unitarian Association and testified to his conversion to Unitarianism. He went on and "stated the needs of his church, and the Unitarians took a collection, which totaled $49. A few dollars were added to this amount and he was sent on his way." Douglas Stange reports this happening in his book *Patterns of Antislavery Among American Unitarians, 1831-1860,* and concludes, "No discussion, no welcome, no expression of praise and satisfaction was uttered, that the Unitarian gospel had reached the 'colored.'"[1]

It was not an auspicious beginning. And while we may be aghast at the way Mr. Jackson was treated, it should come as no great surprise when one understands the full context. Who were these men (and they were all men) who sent him on his way? Earl Morse Wilbur writes that the early Unitarians in New England "were disposed to be complacent and self-confident, and felt moved by no eager desire to make converts to their religion or to urge it upon others." While there were some youthful ministers who were eager and zealous to form an association to help spread the faith, others were cautious like William Ellery Channing, while still others believed that Unitarianism should be propagated slowly and silently, for they "feared Unitarianism would become popular, and when it was in the majority would become intolerant."[2]

In the light of early Unitarian reluctance to spread liberal Christianity even among others like themselves, their disinclination to do mission work except through the Society for the Propagation of the Gospel Among Indians and Others in North America, their belief that the Negro was innately inferior—a belief Channing and Parker shared—and the horror with which Unitarians universally viewed the possibility of racial amalgamation, one would expect no other response than the one received by the Rev. Mr. Jackson.

This attitude toward spreading our faith differed markedly from that of the Baptists and the Methodists. Their believers led revivals in the North and South for both white and black people. Those concerned with the saving of souls pressed on with an urgency with which the religious liberal was unfamiliar.

Yet there were religious liberals who had a grander vision of their faith. One was the famous Universalist "grasshopper missionary" Quillen Shinn, who saw the possibility of spreading the faith among black people. During the 1890s and into the twentieth century, he gave his full support to the congregations and mission schools in Virginia. He also made an attempt in Georgia and at one point hoped to build a theological school to train black Universalist ministers. In time all these churches failed and the dream languished, but the reasons for their failure, which I will not explore here, were quite different from those that underlie Unitarianism's failure.

There were Unitarians who had vision, as well. One was the Rev. Jenkin Lloyd Jones who, when he became minister of All Souls Unitarian Church in Chicago in 1882, set out to form a "church which must emphasize Universal Brotherhood." Indeed, a black member of his congregation, Mrs. Fannie Barrier Williams, delivered an address at the 1893 World Parliament of Religions entitled "The Religious Mission of the Colored Race." And when Jones created the Abraham Lincoln Centre in 1905 as a new home for the Chicago All Souls Church, he envisioned "a great community . . . at the heart of which should be the interracial, non-sectarian church."[3] Another visionary was the Rev. Franklin C. Southworth, the President of Meadville Theological School from 1902 to 1927, who saw that the school had a role "in solving the race problem," and enrolled a succession of black men—Don Speed Smith Goodloe, James Thompson Simpson, and then Egbert Ethelred Brown. John Haynes Holmes, the minister of the Community Church of New York, was yet another who addressed the problem of race in America. In 1909 he was among the founders of the NAACP and soon thereafter he saw to it that his own congregation became integrated. These ministers were the exception, the handful who had a vision of a non-white Unitarian movement.

I argue in previous chapters that Unitarianism has made so few inroads into the black community because it has not spoken to the black experience. But, as I continue to analyze why there are so few African American Unitarian Universalists, I have come to believe that the more fundamental obstacle has been an arrogance that has limited our vision. So self-satisfied were we that we couldn't imagine attracting many, save others who were like us "but didn't know it."

The reality of our situation was that there were more opportunities than there were visionaries in places of influence. In 1912 not only had Ethelred Brown returned from training at Meadville Theological School to take up his ministry in Jamaica, but there also existed the Sierra Leone Unitarian Christian Church in West Africa. These were opportunities, but today they are both just history. The ensuing decades were even more symptomatic of Unitarianism's lack of vision. Our leaders were simply unwilling to reach out to those who did not fit our mold.

The three and a half decades of Brown's struggle is the most poignant example, but just one of many. The welcome

Lewis McGee received in 1927 when he traveled to Chicago and spoke with Curtis Reese, was one of discouragement. Inspired by *Humanist Sermons*, a book Reese had edited, McGee inquired about becoming a Unitarian minister. Reese, who was then Dean of the Abraham Lincoln Centre, replied, "If you want to become a Unitarian minister, you'll have to bring your own church." Twenty years later that is what McGee had to do—he founded his own church, The Free Religious Fellowship.

Jeffrey Campbell, a 1935 graduate of the Canton Theological School of St. Lawrence University, was accepted into Fellowship as a Universalist in the same year and as a Unitarian in 1938. He served as a field secretary to the Student Christian Movement, but later was caught in England during the Second World War. When he returned he remained unable to find a parish settlement despite his constant approaches to denominational officials. He recalled that the AUA President, Frederick May Eliot, "would start making excuses as soon as he saw me at the other end of the corridor."[4] His first settlement finally came in 1967, when he was called as the part-time minister in Amherst, Massachusetts.

In 1938 Felix Lion, a Unitarian minister then just out of school and working for the summer in Cincinnati, accidently discovered a little storefront church named "The Church of the Unitarian Brotherhood." Its founder, William H. G. Carter, grew up on a farm in Arkansas, attended Shorter College, discovered the idea of Unitarianism through his own reading, and created the Brotherhood Church in 1918. Carter, when interviewed in 1936, believed that it was "the only colored Unitarian Church in the United States."[5] It was not, but in predating Brown's effort in Harlem by two years, it was the first.

Carter was a "prominent Negro leader"[6] and the Unitarian ministers in Cincinnati knew of him, but, believing the church to be in the wrong neighborhood, had never informed the AUA. When the AUA did send someone to interview Carter, it was reported that the ministers of the other Unitarian Churches in Cincinnati who had spoken there found "the reaction . . . was not very intelligent." The report went on to say that "the neighborhood around the storefront church is poor and characterized by rowdiness. There are several storefront sects within two blocks."[7] The Rev. Lon Ray Call, who submitted the report, wrote in response to my inquiry about Carter, " . . . sorry if I kept a good man from fulfilling his mission."[8] Call also explained that Unitarianism had been in a decline since 1900, losing 240 churches between 1900 and 1930, and that discouraging such marginal endeavors was a matter of policy. In this case, given the state of the AUA, perhaps the decision made sense, but the pattern of rejection experienced by black ministers tells us it was something else as well; there was no vision. I recall a conversation with a long-time friend of my family, a black physician. He told me that he had had a classmate in college who years later told him he had started a Unitarian church. I didn't recognize the name, and perhaps he misunderstood what he had heard, but it made me wonder how many people came up with the idea on their own. How many indigenous, black, storefront, Unitarian churches may have existed about which we have never known and could not imagine?

This was an era during which a number of Unitarians were at the forefront of the humanist movement, but "Oh my God, a storefront Unitarian church," how outrageous!

Godless religion was more acceptable than Godly religion preached in the wrong place, in the wrong way. We knew what a Unitarian church was supposed to be like, and in that preconceived notion there was no room for a store-front church or religion that might be too outwardly emotional, or some other church that could bring some other new permutation of the liberal gospel. We were smug and comfortable. Blinders of arrogance kept us looking straight ahead. Our vision was stretched to its limit in embracing the humanists: individuals who were of the same class, held similar values, argued with the same vocabulary. But a wider vision of something grander and more inclusive, of a religion that could be philosophically and culturally diverse, was too much. Perhaps it was simply too threatening. It might have changed the religion that we were comfortable with and made us change, too. However, times did change, and so did we.

In 1967 Unitarian Universalists were among the first to respond to the cries of suffering and rage emanating from the African American community. The cries were not new, but, uttered from within the violence and chaos that swept through urban areas of the United States that summer, they held our attention. The UUA's Commission on Race and Religion sponsored the Emergency Conference of Unitarian Universalist Response to the Black Rebellion. The Emergency Conference was held in New York City and attended by approximately 140 people. It began on October 6, 1967 but did not go as planned. Thirty of the thirty-seven African Americans attending withdrew from the planned agenda and moved to another room to hold their own conference. During this meeting the Black Unitarian Universalist Caucus (BUUC) was formed. When the BUUC rejoined those who had remained in the Emergency Conference, it presented a list of non-negotiable demands to the Conference participants. One of these was the establishment of a Black Affairs Council (BAC) whose membership would be chosen by BUUC and would be funded by the UUA for four years at $250,000 a year. After a heated and emotional debate, the Conference affirmed the Caucus' requests.

In February 1968, a National Conference of Black Unitarian Universalists was held in Chicago. There the Black Affairs Council (BAC) was elected. It included black and white members, all chosen by the Black Unitarian Universalist Caucus. As Betty L. Reid later wrote, "Night found me exhausted, unable to sleep, crying with the sadness of the days which must follow and joy of witnessing the new birth of blackness . . . for the sadness of the white liberal, whose work in past years has allowed the first stages of our blackness to occur . . . and the rejection of them now and the puzzlement, the fear, yes, and the pride they feel at our release. I cry for them."[9]

Following that conference, the Community Church of New York, with its long-standing commitment to a vision of an integrated society, served as a catalyst for the formation of another group. In May a group of blacks and whites, calling itself the Black and White Alternative— later changed to Black and White Action (BAWA)—began proposing a process in which blacks and whites would work together to eliminate racism.

A month later, the UUA General Assembly met in Cleveland, Ohio. The Black Affairs Council funding proposal was placed on the agenda. In an atmosphere of extraordinary emotional tension, the proponents of BAWA and BAC competed and struggled for the support of the delegates. On the third day of the Assembly the delegates voted 836 to 327 to fund the Black Affairs Council at $250,000 a year for four years. Later, the delegates voted to give $50,000 to the Black and White Action group. BAC protested.

Following the General Assembly, it was discovered that all of the UUA's unrestricted endowment funds had been spent. There was not sufficient money to fund the Association's current operations and program. The commitment to fund BAC and BAWA, however, was not rescinded.

The UUA had already taken its stand before activist James Forman delivered "The Black Manifesto" on May 4, 1969, a manifesto which demanded reparation from the Euro-American community. But our well-intentioned act of conscience and the quickness of our response were not enough to spare us emotional turmoil and institutional upheaval which intensified in the years that followed.

At the 1969 General Assembly, BAC came in demanding that the agenda as planned be removed by vote of the delegates and a new agenda formed and ordered by BAC/BUUC and FULLBAC (white supporters of full funding of BAC) be substituted. In an uncharacteristically bitter debate, the Assembly delegates refused to accept this procedure. In response to the rebuff, a substantial number of delegates who had supported this demand walked out and regrouped at the nearby Arlington Street Church.

It appeared that a denominational split would occur. Mediation was successful, however, and the Assembly delegates came back together. By a narrow majority of 798 to 737, the delegates voted to support the Black Affairs

Council but not the Black and White Action group.

Following the 1969 General Assembly, a new UUA administration assumed office, and the UUA's financial crisis became its major concern. In an effort to balance the budget, the Board adjusted the BAC appropriation from $250,000 per year for four years to $200,000 over five years. Later it reconsidered, but voted not to restore the original schedule. The Black Affairs Council then disaffiliated itself from the UUA and launched its own funding campaign. In 1970 BAC was dropped from the UUA budget.

The black empowerment controversy was a denominational tragedy. Social and institutional realities placed tremendous pressures on the UUA. The different choices made by many good people set them ideologically and then emotionally in opposition to one another. The pain was so great that we as a denomination recoiled from the "Empowerment Controversy," and a legacy of distrust lingers still.

What I learned as I wept and despaired over the fate of our black pioneers is that there will be other opportunities. They will come again as they have in the past. Our challenge today is to develop a vision that is grand enough and hopeful enough to accept what the present has brought us and what the future shall bring us.

I grew up in the First Unitarian Church of Chicago, and I'm familiar with All Souls in Washington, DC, and the Community Church of New York. All are thoroughly integrated in every aspect of their programs, and I have always hoped that more of our churches could be like them. But I have come to see that that is too narrow a vision. It leaves us with one model, one vision. It assumes that diversity can legitimately come in only one way, but today, as I look about our denomination, I see it coming in many different forms.

In Boston there is the "Church of the United Community" that the UUA and the United Church of Christ assist. It is a thoroughly mixed church but in a way that is very different from the others. It has welfare mothers and ties to labor unions, Puerto Ricans, African Americans, Africans, and whites; the common theme that draws them together is a call to social witness. In Tulsa, Oklahoma, and Decatur, Georgia, there are new congregations which are self-consciously Afrocentric. In California there exists a Korean congregation that grew from the First Unitarian Church of Los Angeles. In one issue of the Unitarian Universalist *World* magazine, the Rev. Hyun Huan Kim, the minister of the Korean Seed Church of Anaheim, challenges us to take our message to the Third World. Will we accept that challenge? Can we embrace this vision? Do we really want to spread the Unitarian Universalist Gospel?

I hope the future that awaits us is not a homogeneous religious liberalism where we differ more in theology than in class, race, and values—our infrequent but familiar and acceptable pattern of interracialism in which each church has a smattering of this group and that. Rather, the vision that I believe will carry us forward is one in which we will have culturally diverse congregations, each adapting religious liberalism in its own way. In this model our religion will be a rich tapestry presenting a simple truth all can grasp. Doubtlessly we will have to adjust, hear new things, and know discomfort while we grow, but we will also experience a revitalization of our faith.

Since that day in 1860 when the Rev. Mr. Jackson walked into the Autumnal Conference of the AUA, we have resisted this. Indeed, in our smugness and arrogance we have been unable to see the issue at all. We were unable or unwilling to see that we would have to change if we were to become a church with a broader, more universal appeal. Perhaps underneath all our protestations of pluralism and all our rhetoric about being the Church Universal, we have all along feared what that would really mean—change.

It is not shameful, but natural, to fear change. I know I do. But it is shameful to be overcome by fear, and behind my black face I, too, blush. The question is how to deal with our fear. For I think our arrogance is a cover for fear. The answer is to give ourselves over to a vision and be seized by it. Being possessed by a vision will enable us to endure and mature.

I am seized by a vision of Unitarian Universalist churches in Jamaica, Sierra Leone, and Harlem (again); of congregations made up of Korean, Hispanic, French Canadian, gay, and interracial members; of communities composed of all shades of theology, with all forms of music; of societies housed in all kinds of buildings from stately King's Chapel to funky storefronts; and most importantly, of all sorts of individuals who, like you and me, are devoted to this faith.

David Baumbaugh has written a benediction which evokes for me this central theme of our faith, and which my wife and co-minister Donna and I use at the close of every service. As I think of his words I look about my religious community, and I see friends and strangers, males and females, black, brown, and white faces, the old and the young, the gay and the straight, the physically challenged—a rich tapestry of individuals—and then I say:

May this church be dedicated to the proposition that beneath all our differences, and behind all our diversity there is a unity which makes us one and binds us forever together in spite of time and death and the space between the stars. Let us pause in silent witness to that unity.

Sometimes in those faces I see a vision, and in the silence I feel a unity and I am sustained.

Chapter Seven

How Open Is the Door?
How Loud Is the Call?

I remember preaching at the Community Church of New York a few years ago. Looking out at the congregation I saw black faces, and felt oddly at home. In Rochester, New York, where I was then the minister, I thought I felt at home, but standing before this congregation was different. Here were people who could identify naturally with my experience as an African American. There were struggles I didn't have to explain and experiences I didn't have to interpret. And being one among many, I was not the sole voice of authority on all black issues. What a relief.

My life as a Unitarian Universalist began in 1952 when a colleague of my father's took us to the First Unitarian Society of Chicago. By 1957 I became a curly-haired, sweet-voiced soprano in the congregation's choir, which had been created by the Reverend Christopher Moore a year earlier. Today that choir is the multiracial Chicago Children's Choir, but back then when I looked across the hall, what I saw was just one other black face, an alto, a pigtailed girl. Often when I looked at her, I would remember that we were different from everyone else.

Growing up black in a white world awakened an acute sense of self-consciousness. In 1960 a group of choir members were chosen to sing with the Chicago Lyric Opera. We were to be altar boys in a production of *Tosca*. Besides singing we had to learn where and how to stand, on which knee to genuflect, how to properly cross ourselves, and how to bear the incense. It was all new, especially the mysterious Catholic rituals. On the night of the dress rehearsal the adults struggled to contain our energy. They managed to get us dressed, and then they put make-up on all the boys except me. The other boys were white, and we were told it was to keep their faces from shining. No one knew what to do about me; and all I knew was that if make-up was part of the show, I didn't want to be left out. I pouted, so at the last moment they let me put on my own. When the word came back later that I'd looked like a clown in whiteface, the make-up also covered my red face. I went without for the rest of the performances.

I can understand the sense of isolation and loneliness that Unitarian Universalists who are non-European Americans feel, and I experience the yearning to be a multicultural church. I also understand that demographically this nation is rapidly changing—becoming more Hispanic, African American, and Asian. This means that we Unitarian Universalists are becoming an increasingly irrelevant remnant of our Boston-bound past. It is clear to me that white members want the Unitarian Universalist Association (UUA) to change.[1] But I wonder if they understand why change has been so difficult. And I doubt that they really understand what that change will mean.

As a denomination we don't understand, and that is why we must examine how some congregations—our most interracial ones—became that way. Why did they succeed?

The door to Unitarianism was first opened to African Americans early in the twentieth century by John Haynes Holmes, minister of the Community Church of New York.

Holmes was among the founders of the National Association for the Advancement of Colored People, the NAACP, in 1909. Donald Harrington, currently minister emeritus of the Community Church, reports that Holmes, his predecessor, had decided "to integrate his lily white church. When no black people came, he asked some of his associates in the NAACP to join his church. 'I don't care what your denomination is,' he told them, 'I want you to come and join us, and teach brotherhood to my people.' The first Black to join was made an usher, standing near the door on the main aisle where he could be easily seen. More and more black people came, and stayed . . ."[2]

One such associate was Agustus Granville Dill, business manager of the *Crisis*, the magazine of the NAACP. Dill "sometimes played the organ for services," and it was he who suggested that Langston Hughes read his poetry at Community Church. It was the first time Hughes, then still a young man, had ever been invited to read his poetry in a church. In 1948 when Community called Maurice Dawkins, an African American graduate of Union Theological School, to be their Minister of Education, they were already well established as a multiracial church.

In Chicago integration happened somewhat differently. Like Holmes, Leslie Pennington, minister of the First Unitarian Society of Chicago, was involved in the issue of race relations and wanted to integrate his church. But unlike Holmes, Pennington "did not feel justified in going out deliberately to find Negroes who would consent to join a Unitarian Church."[3] It was 1947 and they had no African American members. What they did have was a core of members who understood that "'whites only' was never carved over the door of any white Protestant church in

America; it was understood."[4] There was a sense that something had to be done, so at a congregational meeting in January 1948, the members voted, "Be it resolved that we, the members of the First Unitarian Society, do take it upon ourselves to invite our friends of other races and colors who are interested in Unitarianism to join our church and to participate in all its activities, pledging ourselves to seek to become one with them even as we ask them to become one with us."[5]

This seems straightforward enough, but the resolution had already precipitated a major conflict within the congregation's Board of Trustees. One meeting had gone late into the night as they argued over whether or not to integrate. Finally, in the early hours of the morning, one of the trustees, who adamantly opposed integration, was asked: "What is the purpose of the church?"[6] And he blurted out, "To change people like me." He and another trustee later left the church.

The resolution set the First Unitarian Society on its way. The door was open, but in 1948 only one person of color joined, in 1949 another. My own family appeared in 1952. Within the next decade the church membership grew to ten percent African American. And by the time the Reverend Marshall Grigsby, a young, black, birthright Unitarian Universalist, was called as assistant minister in 1970, the congregation was nearly twenty percent black.

It is interesting to note that in both New York City and Chicago, black Unitarian churches emerged almost simultaneously with the efforts of these two large white churches to integrate—an illusive sign that the time was ripe for change. In 1920 the Reverend Ethelred Brown founded the Harlem Unitarian Church, and in 1947 the Reverend Lewis McGee helped found the Free Religious Fellowship of Chicago's south side. Both ended up competing with the Community Church and First Unitarian for members. The larger white churches successfully integrated, but only the Free Religious Fellowship barely survives today.

In 1954, the American Unitarian Association's Committee on Intergroup Relations issued a report titled "How Open Is the Unitarian Door?" They noted that only thirteen churches had five or more Negro members. These churches were almost exclusively large urban churches in cities such as Pittsburgh, Los Angeles, and Detroit. The Community Church of New York was among them as was First Unitarian of Chicago. The Commission found, however, that a majority of Unitarian churches did not feel a special need or desire to attract non-white members. Thus, the Commission stated that "an 'Open Door' policy is not one unless all perceive it to be so." It recommended that the American Unitarian Association (AUA) and its member churches be more intentional and aggressive in their efforts to integrate. It would take nearly a decade before the 1963 UUA General Assembly would pass a resolution requiring new societies to "welcome all qualified persons, regardless of race, color, or place of national origin."[7] Existing congregations were exempted from the requirement.

Among the thirteen congregations with a significant African American presence was All Souls Church in Washington, DC. In the 1950s, All Souls found itself in the midst of a changing neighborhood. White people fled to the suburbs, then the black middle class also moved out, and more and more of the working class and poor arrived in the community. James Reeb and Duncan Howlett, ministers of All Souls, decided that it was paramount they address the needs of the emerging community. Reeb later became a martyr for the civil rights movement when he was clubbed to death by a racist in Selma, Alabama; and Howlett would serve as the first chair of the United States Commission on Civil Rights.

When it was time for Howlett to retire, he decided that All Souls needed an African American minister. The Reverend David Eaton, a Methodist minister who was theologically a Unitarian—and had considered at one time becoming a Unitarian—was approached. He was called to the ministry of All Souls in 1969. In an interview Eaton recalls those first years:

> All Souls was maybe ninety-five percent Euro[pean] American and five percent African American. . . . Around 1970, working with the Board of Trustees, we set out as one of the missions of the church to make it an all inclusive congregation . . . during the period [from] 1970 to 1975 we purposefully attempted to make this a multiracial congregation . . . ; we worked at it. We lost a significant [number] of members—I would say a couple of hundred . . . [who] found it difficult to deal with some of the problems that came with being a multiracial congregation—it wasn't just something that was easily done.[8]

In an award-winning sermon entitled "Racism is Alive and Well," Eaton recounts a telling incident:

> A woman, sixty-two years old, came to my office. She was crying, and I went over and held her in my arms.
>   She said, "I've got to leave the church."
>   I asked, "Why?"

She said, "I'm just not comfortable anymore. It was all right before, with ministers who were white. There were a few blacks, but now there are too many joining the church. I'm not comfortable anymore. I feel ashamed of myself." She said, "I'm liberal, and I never thought that I could have racist feelings, but I do."

I said, "Well, you can try and change."

She said, "No, I'm too old for that, I can't change. When I go to church I want to be comfortable. But I'll send you money from time to time to help the church out." And she left.

I see her from time to time. She is out in one of the suburban churches. I see her through the corner of my eye and if she sees me before I see her, she vanishes quickly; and I let her.

But if I see her first, she smiles and we hug each other, and she asks how things are, and we quickly part. But I appreciate her honesty.[9]

No, it is not easy to be a multiracial church, and the goal is something too many pursue naively.

What can we learn from these three congregations, which successfully opened their doors, and attracted black people? There are five common ingredients:

First, Community Church, First Unitarian, and All Souls were all in large urban areas. Why is this significant? In a book entitled *American Mainline Religion*, Wade C. Roof and William McKinney analyze the demographic structure and value orientation of America's denominations. They state that while once "family and group ties overshadowed religious preference . . . , [today] geographic mobility . . . [has] weakened ties—to family and kin, to neighborhood and community. . . ."[10] Their research indicated that "living in urban areas, in the Northeast and

West, and having moved away from the state in which one was reared were associated with interracial worship. . . ."[11] Thus, one would expect that Unitarian Universalism would attract more black individuals in larger urban areas where familial ties are weaker, communal bonds looser, and the social repercussions for non-conformity less severe. In fact, we know from a survey entitled "The Quality of Religious Life in Unitarian Universalist Congregations," which was released by the UUA Commission on Appraisal (COA) in 1989, that a majority of African American Unitarian Universalists live in large cities, primarily in the Northeast.

Second, a large black middle class is necessary. Let us not fool ourselves. Ours is an upper middle-class religion. Again in *American Mainline Religion*, Unitarian Universalists are cited as having the highest level of education, the highest income, and the highest status of jobs of any denomination.[12] African Americans in our congregations are not different demographically. The COA study indicates that income and educational levels among black Unitarian Universalists are slightly higher than the average—that is higher than the average of the highest denomination in the US. Note that all three of these congregations exist in cities with a large African American middle class and attract black professionals.

Third, the minister and congregation need to be visibly and vocally concerned with issues of race relations and justice so that the church becomes identified as a people who are concerned with the African American agenda. This was the case at Community Church, All Souls, and First Unitarian. Reinforcing this point is the COA study, which shows that seventy-five percent of black Unitarian

Universalists rate social concern as important in the life of a congregation, while only thirty-four percent of white Unitarian Universalists rate it so.

Fourth is intentionality. Each of these congregations took specific action to open its doors.

Fifth and finally, it took time.

Thus, creating a multiracial church requires a large urban area, an African American middle class, visibility in the larger community as an advocate for racial justice, intentionality, and time. To distill this still further, it requires opportunity and commitment.

As a historian of the black experience within Unitarian Universalism, I have tried to discern these patterns so that we might learn from them, but they are still theories which need testing. On March 5, 1990, the second article of five in a series entitled "Hard Choices in Black and White" appeared in the *Washington Post*.[13] This particular article was about the Church of the Restoration, a Unitarian Universalist congregation in Philadelphia. As I read it, phrases which support my theory leaped out: The Church is located in Philadelphia, an urban area comparable to New York City, Washington, DC, or Chicago. The East Mount Airy neighborhood is full of "streets mixed with black and white professionals—teachers, professors, consultants, computer scientists—who are middle class and liberal."[14] The Church of the Restoration has been actively concerned with racial issues since 1965 when its minister, Rudy Gelsey, "flew to Selma for the historic voting rights marches."[15] Later the congregation helped form "a Philadelphia to Philadelphia exchange to start a dialogue among Black and White in the small namesake Mississippi town where three civil rights workers had been killed. They

worked with a watchdog agency tracking local police
brutality allegations . . . [and] they formed the biracial
East Mount Airy Neighbors Association to fight . . . block-
busting. . . ."[16] The congregation is still intentional about
integration under the leadership of Bob Throne, its present minister, who has endeavored "to move it toward
multiculturalism in service and tone, not just in numbers."[17] African American membership increased from a
family or two to several dozen, and today thirty-five of its
one hundred members are black. Finally, Restoration has
weathered the test of time. It survived hard times when
the congregation "stumbled along as an interracial church
but it was a different place: subdued and withdrawn."[18]
But it is that way no longer.

When we consider these four congregations, we can
observe how times change. What worked in New York in
1909 wouldn't have been acceptable in Chicago in 1949. It
took something altogether different in Washington, DC, in
1969, and today in the 1990s the Church of the Restoration
finds itself taking a different tack than it did during the
1960s. As David Eaton reminds us, "It just wasn't something that was easily done." I would like to suggest why it
may be more difficult today.

Our values, in part, define who we are as Unitarian
Universalists. Roof and McKinney's research in *American
Mainline Religion* shows that Unitarian Universalist attitudes on issues of civil liberties, women's rights, racial
justice, and new morality (by which they mean attitudes
toward issues like premarital sex and homosexuality) are
consistently and significantly more liberal than any other
denomination.[19] Christian Scientists, Jews, and the unaffiliated hold views similar to ours, while black denomina-

tions, along with conservative and fundamentalist Protestants, have the least similar views. The only denominations whose values are to the right of black denominations are conservative Protestants, and not only do our values differ from the individuals who attend conservative and black churches, but their members show by far the most institutional commitment. This reality suggests that we couldn't drag many African Americans through our doors if we tried because many of them would disagree with us on central issues of belief, and they have no desire to leave their churches anyway. Not only are we very different from the majority of black Protestants in terms of race, class, and education, but our values are vastly different as well.

Still, there are African Americans who respond to the message of our liberal faith. What we have not understood is that we must compete for them. When asked why she went to the predominantly black UU Free Religious Fellowship instead of the First Unitarian Society of Chicago, Fern Gayten, an African American and one of the founding members of the Fellowship, expressed this sentiment, "We had an obligation to stay where we were and cast down our bucket."[20] This sense of obligation is a strong motivation, and it is why we must compete with such liberal black and interracial churches as Glide Memorial in San Francisco, Allen Temple in Oakland, and Trinity in Chicago. These congregations are located in major cities where we would expect them to be, attract the black middle class, and are concerned with racial justice; but in addition, they are part of the black community. They provide a way for black professionals, who may be living in the suburbs and working in white firms, to be involved in a black institution, to be connected to other black people, to honor their black heritage, and to contribute to a better future by serving as role models for black youth and working for social justice. These issues are of such overriding importance to many individuals that they will accept a theology with which they may not be in complete agreement.

The reality within our denomination is that only a handful of our congregations have experienced significant integration. Our situation tends to bear out Roof and McKinney's findings that "of all divisions among the churches, the color line is the most rigid and enduring." It would serve us well to heed their conclusion that "Protestantism is fundamentally divided along lines of race and liberal-conservative ideology . . ."[21] by developing realistic expectations.

Perhaps a final observation will reveal the magnitude of the challenge. The woman whom David Eaton consoled raised the issue of comfort: "I'm just not comfortable anymore. . . . It was all right before with a white minister and a few Blacks, but now there are too many. . . ."[22] The same thing happened in Chicago and in Philadelphia; white people departed. This may surprise white Unitarian Universalists, but black Unitarian Universalists often feel this way when attending a predominantly white church. The difference is that black people are used to feeling somewhat uncomfortable. Think about what would make a Unitarian Universalist congregation comfortable for you if you were an African American. What would it look like? How would we treat each other? And what would the worship service be like?

To begin with there are simply too many white people in our congregations for blacks to feel as comfortable as we would like—after all the UUA is ninety-seven percent white. African Americans are tired of being the tokens to which white Unitarian Universalists point when trying to prove their liberality. We are tired of dealing with stereotypes that most European Americans have absorbed, and don't want to have to deal with the awkwardness of interracial relations.

Moreover, African American Unitarian Universalists would like a style of worship that we can feel at home with—a style that would culturally express the black experience. The "Quality of Religious Life" study shows that black members differ dramatically from white members when it comes to worship. Unitarian Universalists continue to rank "intellectual stimulation" as the "most important" aspect of worship—seventy-five percent say this, and that has not changed in three decades. Only forty-seven percent of black Unitarian Universalists rate "intellectual stimulation" as "most important."

Among African American Unitarian Universalists, "celebrating common values," "hope," "fellowship," and "music" all rated higher. As Pat DeBrady, a member of Restoration said: "Sometimes I need to know how the eagle stirs its nest," which she later had to translate for a white member of the congregation: "The emotive can be as important as the intellectual."[23] Thirty-six years earlier the Reverend Ethelred Brown expressed the same sentiment to his Unitarian colleagues: "Religion is ethics touched by emotion. If the intellect dominates and there is no hint of emotion, a cold and barren matter-of-factness results."[24] The reality is that Unitarian Universalist congregations simply don't offer the warmth, emotion, and joyous music that would enable African Americans to feel more at home among us. We offer other things, but not these. Most

African Americans must believe that it is not worth the sacrifice to join.

The black individuals we have attracted are the religiously earnest but uncommitted, who are comfortable in an interracial setting and who believe a liberal religious, non-creedal theology and freedom of conscience is more important than racial solidarity or cultural comfort: people who are ready to make this particular compromise and willing to wrestle with an institution like the UUA to make it a place in which other African Americans might feel at home.

As one who has made this compromise, I can understand the yearning of black members in our congregations to have other African Americans march through our doors and fill up our pews. I can understand the desire to have the liberal religious message of freedom and love heard by more people. And I can understand those who fear change. One should. It is difficult.

To move forward as a denomination, we need first to ask ourselves why. I think there is only one authentic answer. For yourself. For yourself because you will feel more comfortable in a multicultural, multiracial congregation. For yourself because being part of an inclusive movement is more consonant with the self-image you hold of yourself as a religious liberal. For yourself so that the piece of you which feels guilty or angry about what "we aren't" can stop feeling guilty and let go of the anger. For yourself because you want the whole world to know about liberal religion. For yourself because you want a style of worship that strikes deeper spiritual cords. For yourself, not because you should, but because you yearn to be different. Not for them but for yourself—ourselves.

For those who choose this direction, know that you are not the first to make this choice. Others have shown the way. But opening the door must be a choice, and sustaining the call takes effort. It will be risky, difficult, and painful, yet we accept such realities when we believe the effort will help us become the people and the place we yearn to be.

Appendix A:
Black Universalist, Unitarian, and Unitarian Universalist Ministers

1. JOSEPH JORDAN (1842-1901)
   Licensed: Universalist—May 1888
   Ordained: Universalist—March 31, 1889
   Settlements: 1887-1889 Norfolk, VA, Minister and
   Founder of the Universalist
   mission
   1889-1901 Norfolk, VA, New Congregation Minister, First Universalist Church of Norfolk

2. THOMAS E. WISE (1868-19?)
   Licensed: Universalist—1894
   Ordained: Universalist—1895
   Settlements: 1889-1901 Norfolk, VA, Assistant Minister, First Universalist Church
   of Norfolk
   1894-1897 Suffolk, VA, Minister and
   Founder of Universalist mission
   1897-1904 Suffolk, VA, New Congregation Minister, St. Paul Universalist Mission
   1901-1904 Norfolk, VA, Building Admin-
   istrator, First Universalist
   Church of Norfolk
   Returned to Methodism 1904

3. JOSEPH FLETCHER JORDAN (1863-1929)
   Education: North Carolina Normal School; Canton

Theological School of St. Lawrence University, 1903-1904; honorary D.D. from Barretts College, NC, 1900; read law and passed North Carolina Bar exam

Fellowshiped: Universalist—March 1904

Ordained: Methodist—December 7, 1889

Settlements: 1902, 1904-1906 Norfolk, VA, Minister, First Universalist Church of Norfolk

1904-1929 Suffolk, VA, Minister, St. Paul Univeralist Mission

1904-1929 Suffolk, VA Principal, Suffolk Normal Training School

4. EGBERT ETHERLRED BROWN (1875-1956)

Education: private grammar school, Jamaica; Meadville Theological School, 1910-1912

Fellowshiped: Unitarian—April 25, 1912; Dropped May 28, 1929; Reinstated May 8, 1935

Ordained: June 1912

Settlements: 1908-1914 Montego Bay, Jamaica, BWI

1914-1920 Kingston Jamaica, BWI

1920-1956 Harlem, NY

5. JEFFREY WORTHINGTON CAMPBELL (1910-1984)

Education: B.A. St. Lawrence University, 1933; B.D. Canton Theological School, 1935

Fellowshiped: Universalist—June 1935; Unitarian— May 1938

Ordained: Universalist—June 2, 1935

Settlements: Never held a full-time church position but served the following churches:

1933-1935 Winthrop, NY, Universalist Student Minister

1967-1974 Amherst, MA, part-time

1970-1980 Brattleboro, VT, Affiliate Minister

1974-1975 Charlestown, NH, Interim
           Minister
1975-1984 Semi-retired teacher, Putney
           School, Putney, VT

6. LEWIS ALLEN MCGEE (1893-1979)
    Education: B.D. Payne Theological Seminary of
              Wilberforce University, 1916; B.A.
              Carthage College, 1936; Meadville Theo-
              logical School, 1946-1947
    Fellowshiped: Unitarian—September 5, 1947
    Ordained: September 1917—Methodist
    Settlements: 1948-1953 Chicago, IL, Free Religious
                    Fellowship
              1953-1958 Springfield, OH, Field Secre-
                    tary of the American Humanist
                    Association
              1958-1961 Los Angeles, CA, Associate
                    Minister, First Unitarian
                    Church
              1961-1962 Chico, CA, Minister, Unitar-
                    ian Fellowship
              1962-1963 Anaheim, CA, Interim Minis-
                    ter, Unitarian Church
              1963-1964 Pasadena, CA, Minister of
                    Education, Throop Memorial
                    Universalist Church
              1965-1966 Bayside, CA, Humboldt
                    Unitarian Fellowship
              November 1966 Minister Emeritus,
                    Humboldt Unitarian Fellow-
                    ship

7. EUGENE SPARROW (1921-1978)
    Education: B.A. University of Michigan, 1946; S.T.B.
              Harvard Divinity School, 1949
    Fellowshiped: Unitarian—June 8, 1949
    Ordained: Unitarian—July 31, 1949

Settlements: 1948-1949 Somerville, MA, Assistant
Minister
1956-1960 Ann Arbor, MI, Minister-at-
Large
1960-62 Director of Field Services,
Midwest UU churches

8. MAURICE A. DAWKINS
Education: B.A. Columbia College, 1944; M.A. Union
Theological School, 1950
Affiliated Fellowship: Unitarian—June 15, 1950
Ordained: Baptist—May 15, 1947
Settlement: 1948-1954 , New York, NY Minister of
Education, Community Church

9. BENJAMIN RICHARDSON (1914-1992)
Education: A.B. Florida A&M University, 1936; S.T.B.
Harvard Divinity School, 1939; Certificate
of Education, Newark State Teachers
College, 1948
Fellowshiped: Unitarian—June 2, 1954; Dropped April
22, 1974
Ordained: Congregational—1940
Settlement: 1954-1962 Chicago, IL, Free Religious
Fellowship
1962-1984 Chicago, IL, Assistant to the
Dean of Liberal Arts and
Sciences, DePaul University;
Joint appointment as pro-
fessor of History and Religious
Studies

10. WILLIAM RONALD JONES
Education: A.B. Howard University, 1955; S.T.B.
Harvard Divinity School, 1958; Ph.D.
Brown University, 1969.
Fellowshiped: Unitarian—June 1958
Ordained: Unitarian—June 1958

Settlements: 1958-1960 Providence, RI, Assistant
Minister, First Unitarian
Church
1969-1977 Yale Divinity School, Assistant Professor
1977-present Tallahassee, FL, Professor,
Florida State University

11. MWALIMU IMARA (née Renford G. Gaines)
Education: B.A. Western Reserve, 1964; D.Min.
Meadville Theological School, 1968
Fellowshiped: Unitarian Universalist—June 4, 1968
Ordained Unitarian Universalist—September 22, 1968
Settlements: 1968-1970 Urbana, IL, Unitarian Church
1970-1974 Boston, MA, Arlington Street
Church
1974-1979 Boston, MA, Minister-at-
Large, Benevolent Fraternity
1979-1983 Indianapolis, IN, Director of
Hospice, Methodist Hospital
1983-1988 Atlanta, GA, Chairman,
Department of Counseling
Services, Morehouse College
1983-present Atlanta, GA, Director,
Human Values in Medicine
Program and Associate Professor of Human Behavior, Department of Psychiatry with
cross appointment in Department of Family Medicine,
Morehouse College
1984-1991, Griffin, GA, Priest-in-Charge,
St. Stephen's Episcopal Church
1988-present Atlanta, GA, Pastoral
Counseling; Consultant to
individuals and systems in
corporate settings.

12. JOHN FRAZIER, JR.
    Education: A.B. Torugaloo College, 1967; B.D. Crane
                Theological Seminary, 1968; M.Div.
                Ashland College, 1971
    Fellowshiped: Unitarian Universalist—June 9, 1968
    Ordained: Unitarian Universalist—July 19, 1969
    Settlements: 1969-1974 Cleveland, OH, UU Humanist
                    Fellowship of Liberation
                 1974-1980 Chaplain, North Carolina
                    Correction Center for Women
                 1980-1984 Senior Policy Advisor for the
                    Governor of North Carolina
                 Currently: President and CEO of Na-
                    tional Telephone Service.

13. THOMAS ELIRON PAYNE
    Education: B.A. Howard University, 1965; B.D., 1968;
                D.Minn.,1975; Th.Min. Harvard Divinity
                School, 1969
    Fellowshiped Unitarian Universalist—July 22, 1968
    Ordained: Unitarian Universalist—May 10, 1970
    Settlements: 1970-1972 Lyons, OH
                 1972-1977 Lucasville, OH, Chaplain,
                    Southern Ohio Correctional
                    Facility
                 1977-1987 Boston, MA, Associate Minis-
                    ter-at-Large, Benevolent
                    Fraternity; Roxbury, MA, Co-
                    minister, First Church
                 1987-89 Norwich, CT, Interim Minister,
                    Unitarian Universalist Church
                 1989-1991 Lexington, KY, Interim
                    Minister, Unitarian Universal-
                    ist Church
                 1992-1993 Chicago, IL, Interim Minister
                 1993-present Columbia, SC, Interim
                    Minister, Unitarian Universal-
                    ist Fellowship

14. HAROLD ANTHONY WILSON
    Education: B.A. San Francisco State; B.D. Thomas
               Starr King School for Religious Leader-
               ship, 1968
    Fellowshiped: Unitarian Universalist—July 7, 1969;
               Dropped September 22, 1975
    Ordained: Unitarian Universalist—June 23, 1968
    Settlement: 1968-1973 Walnut Creek, CA, Co-minis-
                        ter, Mt. Diablo Unitarian
                        Church
                   1973-1980 California Personnel Director
                        and Director of Public Informa-
                        tion Lawrence Berkeley Labo-
                        ratories
                   1980-1981 California, Director of Train-
                        ing and Affirmative Action,
                        Lawrence Berkeley Laborato-
                        ries
                   1981-1987 California Director of Project
                        Management and Education
                        Programs, Lawrence Berkeley
                        Laboratories
                   1987-present California, President and
                        CEO, Nationwide Technologies,
                        Inc.

15. DAVID HILLIARD EATON (1932-1992)
    Education: B.A. Howard University, 1956; S.T.B.
               Boston University, 1959; D.Min, 1972
    Fellowshiped: Unitarian Universalist—May 1972
    Ordained Methodist—April 1957
    Settlement: 1969-1992 Washington DC, Minister, All
                        Souls Unitarian Church

16. HOWARD THURMAN TRAYLOR
    Education: B.A. University of California, 1967; M.Div
               Thomas Starr King School for Religious
               Leadership, 1972

Fellowshiped: Unitarian Universalist—November 12,
        1973; Dropped May 1979

17. EDWARD E. THOMPSON
    Education: M.Div. Thomas Starr King School for
            Religious Leadership, 1975
    Fellowshiped: Unitarian Universalist —February 8,
            1977
    Ordained: Unitarian Universalist—February 8, 1975
    Settlements: 1977-1980 Soledad, CA, Chaplain,
                    Soledad Prison
                1980-1981 San Francisco, CA, Interim
                    Minister, Church for the
                    Fellowship of All Peoples
                1981-1983 Soledad, CA, Chaplain,
                    Soledad Prison
                Resigned: 1983

18. MARK DOUGLAS MORRISON-REED (nee Reed)
    Education: M.A. University of Chicago, 1977; D.Min.
            Meadville/Lombard Theological School,
            1979
    Ordained: Unitarian Universalist—May 6, 1979
    Fellowshiped: Unitarian Universalist—June 10, 1979
    Settlements: 1979-1988 Rochester, NY, Co-minister,
                    First Universalist Church
                1988-present Toronto, ON, Co-minister,
                    First Unitarian Congregation

19. RONALD BRUCE WHITE
    Education: B.A. Yale University, 1967; M.Div. Episco-
            pal Theological School, 1972; M.D. Tufts
            University, 1978
    Ordained: Unitarian Universalist—May 12, 1980
    Settlements: 1979-1981 Roxbury, MA, part-time
                    Assistant Minister, First
                    Church
                1981-present Jamaica Plain, MA,

Assistant Minister, First Church
Currently: Medical Director Brookside Family Health
Center, Jamaica Plain, MA

20. MARSHALL C. GRIGSBY
Education: B.A. Morehouse College, 1968; M.Th.
University of Chicago, 1970;
D.Min., 1972
Fellowshiped: Unitarian Universalist—September 29,
1980
Ordained: Unitarian Universalist—June 20, 1970
Settlements: 1970-1976 Chicago, IL, Assistant Minis-
ter, First Unitarian Church
1973-1976 Vandalia, OH, Associate
Director, American Association
of Theological Schools
1976-1985 Washington, DC, Assistant
Dean and Associate Professor,
Howard University Divinity
School
1985-1993 Columbia, SC, President,
Benedict College
1993-present Hampton, VA, Executive
Vice-president and Provost,
Hampton University

21. YVONNE K. SEON(nee Reed-Chapelle)
Education: B.A. Allegheny College, 1959; M.A. American University, 1960; Ph.D. Union Graduate School, 1974; M.Div. Howard University, 1981
Fellowshiped: Unitarian Universalist:—November 16,
1981
Ordained: Unitarian Universalist—November 21, 1981
Settlement: Washington, DC, Garden of Gethsemane

22. ADELLE SMITH-PENNIMAN
Education: B.A. Bennington College, 1968; M.A.

Columbia University, 1972; M.Div.
Harvard Divinity School, 1979
Fellowshiped: Unitarian Universalist—September
1982
Ordained: Unitarian Universalist—September 12,
1982
Settlements: 1983-present Boston, MA, Co-director,
Women's Theological Center
1986-present Boston, MA, Executive
Director, Women For Economic
Justice

23. T. EWELL HOPKINS
Education: B.A., West Virginia State College, 1933;
B.D., Howard University, 1938; M.A., 1939
Fellowshiped: Unitarian Universalist—May 9, 1983
Ordained: National Baptist Convention, Inc.—1936
Settlement: 1983-present Associate Minister, First
Parish Framingham, MA.

24. MELVIN AUBREY HOOVER
Education: B.S. Ohio State University, 1968; M.Div.
Colgate/Rochester, 1972
Ordained: Episcopal—July 3, 1971
Fellowshiped: Unitarian Universalist—September 24,
1984
Settlements: 1984-1987 Stamford, CT, Executive
Secretary, Council of Churches
1987-1989 Boston, MA, Urban and
International Programs Direc-
tor, Unitarian Universalist
Association
1989-1992 Boston, MA, Advocate for
Racial Inclusivity, Unitarian
Universalist Association
1989-1992 Boston, MA, Director of
International Congregations,
Unitarian Universalist

Association
1992-present Boston, MA, Director of
Racial and Cultural Diversity,
Unitarian Universalist
Association

25. MICHELLE WHITTINGHAM BENTLEY
Education: B.A. University of Illinois, 1973; M.A.
Northeastern Illinois University, 1976;
M.Div. Meadville/Lombard Theological
School, 1986
Ordained: Unitarian Universalist—1986
Settlements: 1987-1989 Chicago, IL, North River
Unitarian Universalist
1988-1989 Chicago, IL, South Loop
Unitarian Universalist
1990-1991 Chicago, IL, Chaplain,
BRASS, Inc.
1991-1992 Chicago, IL, Associate Minis-
ter, First Unitarian Society
1992-1993 Chicago, IL, Interim Senior
Minister, First Unitarian
Society
1993-present Chicago, IL, Dean of
Students and Lecturer,
Meadville/Lombard Theological
School

26. CHARLES JOHNSON
Education: M.Div. Starr King School for the Ministry,
1986
Ordained: Unitarian Universalist—June 28, 1987
Settlement: 1987-present Tulsa, OK, New Congrega-
tion Minister, Church of the
Restoration

27. DANIEL WEBSTER ALDRIDGE, JR.
Education: B.S. Tennessee State University, 1960;

M.Ed. Wayne State University, 1980; M.A.
Ashland Theological Seminary, 1984
Ordained: United Church of Christ—November 29,
1984
Fellowshiped: Unitarian Universalist—May 13, 1988
Settlements: 1989-1994 Decatur, GA, New Congrega-
tion Minister, Thurman Hamer
Ellington Church
1994-present Washington, DC, Minister,
All Souls Unitarian Church

28. TONI VINCENT
Education: B.S. University of Southern California/Los
Angeles, 1960; M.Div. Starr King School
for the Ministry, 1987
Ordained: Unitarian Universalist—January 29, 1989
Settlement: 1991-1993 San Francisco, CA, New
Congregation Minister, New
Community Congregation

29. DONALD E. ROBINSON
Education: B.A. W.Virginia State College, 1962; M.A.
University of the District of Columbia,
1977; M.Div. Howard University Divinity
School
Ordained: Unitarian Universalist—June 17, 1990
Settlement: 1991-present Washington, DC, Director
of Beacon House Community
Ministry, Inc.

30. MARJORIE BOWENS-WHEATLEY
Education: M.A. American University, 1982; M.Div.
Wesley Theological Seminary, 1994
Ordained:Unitarian Universalist—Scheduled for
December 1994

Appendix B:
The African American Unitarian Universalist

Reprinted from "The Quality of Religious Life in Unitarian Universalist Congregations," A Survey by the UUA Commission on Appraisal, 1989.

The Unitarian Universalist Association has not kept statistics on the racial composition of its congregations. The Commission on Appraisal felt that this was important information, so the survey asked individuals to identify their race. The sample of blacks was small (16 people), but it enabled us to make a demographic description of who African American UUs are and to run some cross-tabulations. Our assumption was that African American UUs are similar to other UUs. This is true, but there are also some significant differences.

In 1968 there were about 180,000 Unitarian Universalists and it was estimated that approximately 1500 were black, or less than 1%. In 1987 there were about 140,000 adult UUs and of these 1.3%, or roughly 1800, were black. The same pattern is reflected in the number of black Unitarian Universalist ministers. While their number more than doubled from 7 to 15 between 1968 and 1987, the percentage of African Americans in the UU ministry rose only from a little less than 1% to 1.4%.

The typical African American Unitarian Universalist is a male who lives in a large city in the Northeast and attends a large church. His income and educational level are slightly higher than other UUs, and he is likely to have been reared as a Baptist or Methodist. In socio-economic status the African American UU is very similar to the

Euro-American UU, but the former's attitude toward worship is significantly different.

The table below compares the overall average response to Question 13 (importance of aspects of worship service) with the black response.

	Very Important		Somewhat Important		Not Important	
	Avg	Black	Avg	Black	Avg	Black
Intellectual Stimulation	74%	47%	24%	40%	3%	13%
Fellowship	65%	56%	32%	37%	3%	6%
Celebrating Common Values	60%	69%	35%	12%	5%	19%
Personal Reflection	53%	43%	39%	43%	9%	14%
Group Experience of Participation/Worship	44%	40%	43%	44%	12%	20%
Music	40%	50%	45%	36%	15%	14%
Motivation to Serve Others	30%	31%	53%	56%	17%	13%
Aesthetic Satisfaction	27%	29%	52%	57%	21%	14%
Hope	37%	60%	41%	26%	22%	13%
Vision	35%	46%	43%	46%	22%	8%
Comfort	19%	36%	46%	14%	35%	50%

It is clear that African Americans rank many aspects of worship differently than whites. Intellectual stimulation, which has prevailed historically as the dominant feature of liberal worship, is less highly valued. *Celebrating common values* is most important, and *hope, vision,* and *music* are much more significant aspects of worship for African Americans.

Of the 16 black UUs who responded to Question 32 about God, only one found the term God "irrelevant." The other 15 believe in some form of God. Because of the uniqueness of black spirituality, this striking difference bears on UU discussion of how to increase minority participation.

In terms of beliefs, African American UUs are more likely than average to identify themselves as Christians or Christian-Humanist: 28% as compared to 20%, and are less likely to call themselves Humanist-Existentialist: 36% as compared to 54%. Almost all use the term God and are more inclined to pray.

It is worth noting that while characteristics like being male, highly educated, and having a high income elsewhere are associated with a less "traditional" religious orientation, this does not hold up for African Americans, who appear to be much more religious traditionalists than the average UU.

Question 24 asked respondents to rate factors that contribute to the quality of UU society's life. African Americans rated the importance of *worship* higher than whites, even though their participation is slightly less. The importance of *embracing diversity* was rated high to moderately high by 87% of blacks, as opposed to a general average of 39%. *Social concerns* was rated similarly, 75% to 34%. This is true despite the fact that in the context of the worship service (Question 13) *motivation to serve others* was rated by blacks, as it was by others, as just moderately important.

In response to Question 16, African Americans felt ignored or unwelcome by congregations 25% of the time, while the norm was 10%. Elsewhere, 75% of the blacks involved in UU congregations indicated that they participate in decision-making, while others said this only 62% of the time. When asked if their talents were used, 34% of the respondents said no, and 53% of them blacks. Yet 53% of the African Americans had held an office as opposed to 43% in general. One can't help but be struck by this: African

Americans felt less welcomed and more under-utilized, and yet held more offices and more frequently felt that they participated in decision-making.

Notes

PREFACE

1. "Civil Rights, the Caucus and Separatism," *Unitarian Universalist Register-Leader*, May 1968, p. 4.
2. For a complete list of black Unitarian, Universalist, and Unitarian Universalist ministers and their settlements, see Appendix A.
3. The last comprehensive survey seems to have been that done by Frank S. Loescher and reported in his book *The Protestant Church and the Negro* (New York: Association Press, 1948), p. 77. He wrote that 90 percent of all black churchgoers belonged to black denominations, 10 percent to all-black conventions or churches in white denominations, and one-tenth of 1 percent to churches with a racially mixed membership. There has been slight change over the past thirty-five years, as the more recent figures in the text indicate. Professor Gayraud S. Wilmore, who is currently dean of the Program of Black Church Studies at Colgate Roches-ter Divinity School/Bexley Hall/Crozer, supplied me with this estimate in spring 1982. A number of white denominations have had success in increasing their black membership. Among them is the Reformed Church in America. Noel Leo Erskine has recorded history of this church in *Black People and the Reformed Church in America* (Reformed Church Press, 1978).
4. Homer Jack, "Sunday at 11: Segregation Hour," *Christian Register*, October 1954, p. 15.
5. Robert B. Tapp, *Religion Among the Unitarian Universalists: Converts in the Stepfathers' House* (New York: Seminar Press, 1973), p. 79.
6. William Schulz, "Director for Social Responsibility

Reflects on UU Paradox," *UU World*, March 1, 1979, p.2.
7. Robert Bellah, *The Broken Covenant* (New York: Seabury Press, 1973), p. 3.
8. Stephen Steinberg, *The Ethnic Myth: Race, Ethnicity and Class in America* (Boston: Beacon Press, 1981), p. 255.

1: TWO AMERICAN FAITHS

1. H. Richard Niebuhr, *The Social Sources of Denominationalism*, eleventh edition (New York: World Publishing Co., 1929), p. 6. I have followed Niebuhr closely in this book. First published fifty years ago, Niebuhr's book is a classic and his descriptions are still accurate. In addition, Niebuhr was a contemporary and an associate of Ethelred Brown.
2. Niebuhr, p. 29.
3. Niebuhr, pp. 54-72.
4. Niebuhr, pp. 30-31, 81, 83.
5. James W. McClendon, *Biography as Theology: How Life Stories Can Remake Today's Theology* (Nashville: Abingdon Press, 1974), pp. 35, 37.
6. McClendon, pp. 35, 37-38.
7. McClendon, pp. 96-97.
8. W. E. B. DuBois, *The Souls of Black Folk* (New York: Fawcett, 1961), pp. 147-148.
9. Cecil Wayne Cone, *The Identity Crisis in Black Theology* (Nashville: African Methodist Episcopal Church, 1975), p. 21.
10. Joseph R. Washington, Jr., *Black Religion* (Boston: Beacon Press, 1964), pp. 294, 297.
11. James H. Cone, *God of the Oppressed* (New York: Seabury Press, 1975), pp. 65, 80.
12. James H. Cone, *The Spirituals and the Blues* (New York: Seabury Press, 1972), pp. 34, 17.
13. J. Cone, *Spirituals*, pp. 68, 65.
14. Preston N. Williams, "Black Church: Origin, History, Present Dilemmas," *Andover-Newton Quarterly*, vol. 9,

no. 2 (November 1968): 112.

15. C. Cone, *Black Theology*, pp. 122, 43.

16. McClendon, *Biography*, pp. 75, 82.

17. J. Cone, *Spirituals*, p. 47.

18. C. Cone, *Black Theology*, p. 36.

19. J. Cone, *Spirituals*, p. 48.

20. Frederick Douglass, *Life and Times of Frederick Douglass* (revised edition 1892; reprint, London: Crowell-Collier, 1962), pp. 91-92.

21. C. Cone, *Black Theology*, p. 21.

22. Gayraud S. Wilmore, *Black Religion and Black Radicalism* (Garden City, NY: Doubleday, 1972), p. 226.

23. Martin Luther King, Jr., *Strength to Love* (New York: Pocket Books, 1963), pp. 77-87.

24. W. E. B. DuBois, *The Gift of Black Folk* (1924; reprint, New York: Washington Square Press, 1970), p. 67.

25. Cited by Coretta Scott King, *My Life with Martin Luther King, Jr.* (New York: Holt, Rinehart & Winston, 1969), p. 239.

26. Charles H. Lyttle, *Freedom Moves West* (Boston: Beacon Press, 1952), p. 275.

27. Perry Miller, *Errand into the Wilderness* (Cambridge, MA: Harvard University Press, 1956), pp. 4, 56.

28. Sidney E. Mead, *The Lively Experiment* (New York: Harper & Row, 1963), pp. 39, 36.

29. Thomas Jefferson, *Notes on the State of Virginia*, William Peden, ed. (Chapel Hill: University of North Carolina Press, 1955), p. 161.

30. William Ellery Channing, "The Free Mind," in *Hymns for the Celebration of Life*, Unitarian Universalist Hymnbook Commission, ed. (Boston: Beacon Press, 1966), Responsive Reading no. 420.

31. Kenneth L. Patton, "Let All Who Live in Freedom," in *Hymns for the Celebration of Life*, Unitarian Universalist Hymnbook Commission, ed. (Boston: Beacon Press, 1966), Hymn no. 171.

32. Samuel Longfellow, "O Life That Maketh All Things New," in *Hymns for the Celebration of Life*, Unitarian

Universalist Hymnbook Commission, ed. (Boston: Beacon Press, 1966), Hymn no. 54.

33. Charles Lyttle, "Church of the Free Spirit," in *Hymns for the Celebration of Life*, Unitarian Universalist Hymnbook Commission, ed. (Boston: Beacon Press, 1966), Hymn no. 254.

34. A. Powell Davies, *Man's Vast Future: A Definition of Democracy* (New York: Farrar, Straus and Young, 1951).

35. Niebuhr, *Denominationalism*, p. 87.

36. Vincent Silliman, "Faith of the Free," in *Hymns for the Celebration of Life*, Unitarian Universalist Hymnbook Commission, ed. (Boston: Beacon Press, 1966), Hymn no. 257.

37. Robert L'H. Miller, "The Religious Value System of Unitarian Universalists," *Review of Religious Research*, vol. 17, no. 3 (Spring 1976): 208.

38. Miller, "The Religious Value System," pp. 193-194.

2: A DREAM ABORTED

1. "What the Universalist Church Is Doing, 1907 to 1909," (n.d.), Universalist Collection: Harvard/Andover Divinity School Library, p. 49.

2. Russell E. Miller, *The Larger Hope*, vol. 2 (Boston: Unitarian Universalist Association, 1985), p. 370.

3. George Huntston Williams, *American Universalism* (Boston: Beacon Press, 1971), p. 51.

4. American Unitarian Association, *Unitarian Yearbook 1912* (Boston, 1912), p. 130.

5. Egbert Ethelred Brown, "A Brief History of the Harlem Unitarian Church" (Sermon delivered in the Harlem Unitarian Church, September 11, 1949), Unitarian Universalist Association Archives, Boston, p. 1. All other references to Egbert Ethelred Brown's authorship are given as Brown.

6. "Harlem Pastor Founder of Community Church Works Seven Days a Week as Elevator Boy," *New York Home News*, October 1, 1922, p. 5.

7. Brown, "Brief History," p. 1.
8. "Harlem Pastor," p. 5.
9. Dorice Brown Leslie, interview in Jamaica, New York, on December 4, 1978.
10. Brown, "Brief History," p. 2.
11. Untitled and undated manuscript in Brown, Papers, Schomburg Center for Research in Black Culture, New York Public Library, New York City, pp. 4-5. Astor, Lenox and Tilden Foundations hereafter cited as Schomburg Center.
12. Brown, "Brief History," pp. 2-3.
13. Louis C. Cornish to Kenneth McDougall, October 26, 1921, in Brown, Papers, Unitarian Universalist Association Archives, Boston. Hereafter cited as UUA Archives.
14. Brown, "A Story and an Appeal," *Christian Register*, May 4, 1911, p. 493.
15. Brown, "Brief History," pp. 3-4.
16. There have been at least twelve black students at Meadville Theological School: Alfred Amos Williams, 1871, African Methodist Episcopal (AME) ministry; James Cortland Palmer, 1874, African Methodist Zion Episcopal ministry; Robert Miller Henderson, 1877, AME ministry; William Preston Ross, 1878-1880, AME ministry; Don Speed Smith Goodloe, 1903-1906; James Thompson Simpson, 1909-1910, AME ministry; Egbert Ethelred Brown, 1910-1912, Unitarian ministry; Alvin Neely Cannon, 1943-1944, a Unitarian but never settled; Lewis Allen McGee, 1946-1947, Unitarian ministry; Mwalimu Imara, registered as Renford Gaines, 1964-1968, Unitarian Universalist ministry; Mark D. Morrison-Reed, 1974-1979, Unitarian Universalist ministry; Michelle W. Briggs, 1983, Unitarian Universalist ministry. Compiled from the *General Catalogue of the Meadville Theological School, 1844-1944* and the 1979 *UUA Directory*.
17. Franklin Southworth to Brown, February 4, 1903, in Meadville/Lombard Theological School Archives, Chi-

cago.
18. Wallis A. Goodloe, telephone interview on November 19, 1982.
19. *Who's Who in America*, vol. 9, 1916-1917, p. 962.
20. Leslie, interview.
21. David B. Parke, "Patterns of Power: Universalist and Unitarian Leadership Styles since 1900," *Kairos*, Spring 1976, p.10.
22. Meadville Theological School, "School Notes," in *Quarterly Bulletin*, vol. 6 (June 1912): 18.
23. Brown, "A Statement Presented to the Special Committee Appointed by the American Unitarian Association to Inquire into the Circumstances Leading to the Removal of My Name from the Official List of Unitarian Ministers," December 14, 1931, in Brown, Papers, UUA Archives.
24. Hilary Bygrave, "Report in regard to Montego Bay, etc. Jamaica B.W.I," April 24, 1913, in Samuel A. Eliot, Papers, Andover-Harvard Theological Library, Harvard Divinity School, American Unitarian Association (AUA) Archives, Correspondence, Hilary Bygrave.
25. Brown to Bygrave, June 27, 1913, AUA Archives.
26. Bygrave to Eliot, n.d., AUA Archives.
27. Brown to Walter R. Hunt, March 14, 1926, p. 5, in Brown, Papers, UUA Archives.
28. Brown, "A Statement," p. 1.
29. Dr. Copeland Bowie, secretary of the B & FUA at the time of the Jamaican mission, to Mortimer Rowe, October 23, 1930, Brown, Papers, UUA Archives.
30. Brown, Untitled, pp. 37-42.
31. Brown, "A Statement," p. 2.
32. Brown, Untitled, p. 42.
33. Dorice Brown to the Members of the Unitarian Association, Boston, August 9, 1918, in Brown, Papers, UUA Archives.
34. Arthur C. McGiffert, Jr., *Pilot of the Liberal Faith: Samuel Atkins Eliot, 1862-1950* (Boston: Beacon Press, 1976), pp. 21, 20.

35. McGiffert, *Pilot of the Liberal Faith*, p. 294.
36. Louis C. Cornish to William S. Jones, June 25, 1918, in Brown, Papers, UUA Archives.
37. Cornish to H. Fisher Short, November 23, 1920, in Brown, Papers.
38. Francis E. F. Cornish, *Louis Craig Cornish: Interpreter of Life* (Boston: Beacon Press, 1953), p. 5.
39. Francis E. F. Cornish, *Louis Craig Cornish*, p. 93.
40. Brown, Untitled, pp. 43-44.
41. Brown, "A Statement," p. 2.
42. Ella M. Brown to L. C. Cornish, March 29, 1918, in Brown, Papers, UUA Archives.
43. Brown to Cornish, April 26, 1918, in Brown, Papers, UUA Archives.
44. McGiffert, *Pilot of the Liberal Faith*, p. 17.
45. McGiffert, *Pilot of the Liberal Faith*, p. 107.
46. Brown, "A Statement," p. 2.
47. Dorice Brown to AUA Directors, August 9, 1918, in Brown, Papers, UUA Archives.
48. Brown to Cornish, January 12, 1920, in Brown, Papers, UUA Archives.
49. American Unitarian Association *Unitarian Yearbook 1921-1922* (Boston, 1922), p. 150.
50. James Weldon Johnson, *Black Manhattan* (New York: Knopf, 1930), p. 1.
51. Lerone Bennett, Jr., *Before the Mayflower* (Baltimore: Penguin Books, 1962), p. 297.
52. Brown, Untitled, pp. 47-49.
53. Brown, "Brief History," p. 5.
54. Cornish to McDougall, October 1921, in Brown, Papers, UUA Archives.
55. Brown to George F. Patterson, May 19, 1925, in Brown, Papers, UUA Archives.
56. Brown to George F. Patterson, May 19, 1925, in Brown, Papers, UUA Archives.
57. Brown, Appeal to Unitarian Ministers, November 15, 1926, in Brown, Papers, UUA Archives.
58. Brown to Walter Hunt, March 14, 1926, in Brown,

Papers, UUA Archives.

59. Brown excerpted this in the letter to S. A. Eliot, November 26, 1926, Samuel A. Eliot Papers, AUA Archives, "Bro" file.
60. George Patterson to Fred Lewis, March 8, 1928, in Brown, Papers, UUA Archives.
61. Brown to AUA Directors, November 5, 1928, in Brown, Papers.
62. John Haynes Holmes to Patterson, December 24, 1928, in Brown, Papers.
63. Leslie, interview.
64. AUA, New York (writer unknown), to Walter Hunt, April 1, 1929, in Brown, Papers, UUA Archives.
65. Brown to Frank Wicks, April 12, 1929, in Brown, Papers.
66. Brown to John H. Lathrop, January 9, 1929, in Brown, Papers.
67. Report of the Committee Appointed to Review the Ethelred Brown Case, February 8, 1932, in Brown, Papers, with corrections made April 11, 1932.
68. The quote is taken from a letter (writer and receiver unknown) dated March 1934, in Brown, Papers.
69. Charles Joy, memorandum to Administrative Council, February 1, 1937, in Brown, Papers.
70. Charles Joy to George C. Davis, March 2, 1937, in Brown, Papers.
71. The *World Tomorrow* merged with the *Christian Century* in 1934.
72. Bennett, *Mayflower,* p. 299.
73. Brown, "A Statement," p. 6.
74. Gayraud S. Wilmore, *Black Religion and Black Radicalism* (Garden City, NY: Doubleday, 1972), p. 228.
75. Robert A. Hill, ed., *Marcus Garvey and United Negro Improvement Association Papers*, vol. 1 (Berkeley: University of California Press, 1983), p. 193.
76. Leslie, interview.
77. Brown, *Amsterdam News*, January 6, 1926.
78. *Daily Gleaner*, February 21, 1956.

79. Leslie, interview.
80. W. Adolphe Roberts, "Ethelred Brown: A Tribute," in Brown, Papers, newspaper clippings, no name, no date, Schomburg Center.
81. John H. Lathrop to A. Powell Davies, April 24, 1939, Harlem Unitarian Church Papers, UUA Archives, Boston.
82. Harold Cruse, *The Crisis of the Negro Intellectual* (New York: Morrow, 1967), p. 40.
83. Eugene V. Debs, "The Negro in the Class Struggle," *International Socialist Review*, November 1903, p. 259.
84. Wilson Record, *The Negro and the Communist Party* (New York: Atheneum, 1971), pp. 19,118.
85. Cruse, *Crisis*, p. 40.
86. Brown, "Brief History," p. 7.
87. G. F. Patterson to J. H. Lathrop, November 20, 1930, in Brown, Papers, UUA Archives.
88. Brown to Eliot, November 28, 1930, in Brown, Papers, UUA Archives.
89. Brown, "West Indian-American Relations," *Opportunity*, November 1926, p. 355.
90. Cruse, *Crisis*, p. 120.
91. Randall S. Hilton, secretary, Ministerial Fellowship Committee, summary of interview with Benjamin Richardson, April 26, 1954, in B. Richardson, Papers, UUA Archives, Boston.
92. G. Peter Fleck, telephone interview, in February 1979.
93. Cruse, *Crisis*, p. 46.
94. Marcus Garvey to T. A. McCormack, May 12, 1916, in Hill, ed., *Marcus Garvey*, p. 529.
95. *Amsterdam News*, January 11, 1928, p. 1.
96. Walter Hunt, memorandum of conversation with Mr. Albury, October 15, 1930, in Brown, Papers, UUA Archives.
97. Dale DeWitt, AUA Regional Director, memorandum on the Harlem Unitarian Church, March 4, 1938, in Harlem Unitarian Church Papers.
98. A. Powell Davies, Recommendation from the Commit-

tee on the Field of the Metropolitan Conference to the Church Extension Dept. of the AUA, May 10, 1939, in Harlem Unitarian Church Papers.

99. Brown, "Brief History," p. 7.

100. Brown to Hunt, March 12, 1926, in Brown, Papers, UUA Archives.

101. "Rev. Ethelred Brown Is Symbol of Radicalism in Pulpits in Harlem," *Daily Gleaner*, January 20, 1934.

102. Brown, *Amsterdam News*, n.p., n.d.

103. Brown, "Jesus of Nazareth the World's Greatest Religious Teacher Was a Unitarian," in Brown, Papers, Spingarn Collection, Howard University, Washington, DC.

104. Brown, "My Faith—Then and Now," *Christian Register*, May 1937, p. 715.

105. Brown, "Making Religion More Satisfying Emotionally" (Address delivered at a symposium of the Metropolitan Conference, May 16, 1954), Brown, Papers, Schomburg Center.

106. Brown, "Brief History," p. 88.

107. A. Powell Davies to George C. Davis, May 10, 1939, in Brown, Papers, UUA Archives.

108. Brown to Everett M. Baker, March 4, 1940, in Brown, Papers.

109. See n. 91.

110. Brown, "Brief History," p. 8.

111. Cruse, *Crisis*, p. 428.

112. Brown, Untitled, pp. 55-56.

113. Brown, "Brief History," p. 8.

114. G. C. Davis to Brown, October 22, 1947, in Brown, Papers.

115. G. C. Davis to John Fisher, October 22, 1947, in Brown, Papers.

116. Brown, "A Story and an Appeal," p. 494.

117. Brown to John Haynes Holmes, April 24, 1950, Holmes Correspondence, Library of Congress, Washington, DC.

118. Leslie, interview.

119. Eric Hoffer, *The True Believer* (New York: Harper & Row, 1951; reprint, Perennial Library, 1966), p. 23.
120. Brown, Untitled, p. 55.
121. Brown, address delivered at the celebration of the fortieth anniversary of his ordination, November 30, 1952, in Brown, Papers, UUA Archives.

3: A DREAM PURSUED

1. The Reverend Lewis McGee and Marcella McGee, interview in Bethesda, Maryland, on December 7, 1977, and subsequent telephone conversations and correspondence.
2. Charles V. Hamilton, *The Black Preacher in America* (New York: Morrow, 1972), p. 92.
3. Lewis McGee, "Why I Am a Unitarian," typescript from Marcella McGee, Silver Spring, MD, n.d.
4. John Hope Franklin, *From Slavery to Freedom* (New York: Knopf, 1967), p. 586.
5. Dan Fenn, memorandum to Meadville faculty, April 1946, in Lewis McGee, Papers, Theological School Archives, Chicago.
6. Everett Baker to Wallace Robbins, September 28, 1946, in McGee, Papers.
7. Robbins to George Davis, May 2, 1947, in McGee, Papers.
8. Robert Cummins to Robbins, March 8, 1947, in McGee, Papers.
9. Lewis McGee, "Study of the South Side Negro Community of Chicago, IL" (Commissioned by the American Unitarian Association, Spring 1948) in McGee, Papers.
10. McGee to Robbins, April 30, 1947, in McGee, Papers.
11. Davis to Robbins, May 5, 1949, in McGee, Papers.
12. William Gough, interview in Chicago, Illinois, on February 9, 1979.
13. Kenneth Patton, "A Personal Experience in Brotherhood," *Christian Register*, December 1947, pp. 468-470.
14. Ethelred Brown to Donald Harrington, October 2,

1947, in AUA Integrated Conventions 1940s Papers, UUA Archives.

15. Robbins to Davis, May 2, 1947, in McGee, Papers.

16. McGee to Robbins, April 30, 1947, in McGee, Papers.

17. McGee, "Study," p. 30.

18. William Gough, "History of the Free Religious Fellowship" (typescript).

19. Gough, interview.

20. Waitstill H. Sharp to Dan H. Fenn, August 24, 1949, in Lewis McGee, Papers, UUA Archives.

21. "Twelve Years' Persistence Achieves Integration after Chicago Church Overcomes Slow Start," *Christian Register*, September 1956, p. 26.

22. Donald Harrington, "John Haynes Holmes and the Cry for Social Justice and World Peace" (Sermon delivered at the Community Church of New York on March 16, 1965), published by the Community Church of New York, p. 15.

23. David M. Reimers, *White Protestantism and the Negro* (New York: Oxford University Press, 1965), p. 158.

24. The Reverend Randall Hilton and Gladys Hilton, interview in Chicago, Illinois, on February 7, 1979.

25. Fern Gayten, interview in Chicago, Illinois, on February 8, 1979.

26. Ida Cress, interview in Chicago, Illinois, on February 8, 1979.

27. Harold Cruse, *The Crisis of the Negro Intellectual* (New York: Morrow, 1967), p. 128.

28. Lewis McGee, "A Positive View of Liberal Religion," (Sermon delivered at the Orange County Unitarian Church on January 16, 1953), given to me by Marcella McGee.

29. Gough, interview.

30. Cress, interview.

31. Gayten, interview.

32. "Dawkins Called to Head Los Angeles Church," *Christian Register*, May 1954, p. 30.

33. Virginia Jordan, telephone interview, on November 30,

1982.

34. The Reverend John Morgan, telephone interview, on November 30, 1982.

35. Wilson Tweedee, telephone interview, in December 1982.

36. Lewis McGee to Edwin Wilson, April 17, 1951, in Lewis McGee, Papers, American Humanist Association Archives, Cocoa Beach, FL.

37. Lewis McGee, "Last Word," *FRF Newsletter*, June 17, 1953, p.1.

4: HOW "OPEN" WAS THE DOOR?

1. Earl Morse Wilbur, *A History of Unitarianism in Transylvania, England, and America* (Boston: Beacon Press, 1945), pp. 463-464.

2. Arthur C. McGiffert, Jr., *Pilot of the Liberal Faith: Samuel Atkins Eliot, 1862-1950* (Boston: Beacon Press, 1976), p. 87.

3. "How 'Open' Is the Unitarian Door?" Report of the Commission on Unitarian Intergroup Relations, *Christian Register*, April 1954, p. 11. This report listed the following churches with five or more legal voting black members: Church of the Christian Union, Rockford; First Unitarian Society of Chicago; Free Religious Fellowship, Chicago; Arlington Street Church, Boston; First Church in Roxbury; Church of Our Father, Detroit; Community Church, New York City; Harlem Unitarian Church, New York City; White Plains Community Church, New York; Unitarian Society of Cleveland; First Unitarian Church, Pittsburgh; and All Souls' Church, Washington. One integrated church omitted from the survey was the First Unitarian Church of Los Angeles.

4. "How 'Open' Is the Unitarian Door?" p. 18.

5. Egbert Ethelred Brown, "A Brief History of the Harlem Unitarian Church" (Sermon delivered in the Harlem Unitarian Church, September 11, 1949), UUA Archives, p. 1.

6. Egbert Ethelred Brown, "A Statement Presented to the Special Committee Appointed by the American Unitarian Association to Inquire into the Circumstances Leading to the Removal of My Name from the Official List of Unitarian Ministers," December 14, 1931, in Brown, Papers, UUA Archives.
7. Brown, "The Price I Pay," p. 113.
8. Egbert Ethelred Brown, "My Faith—Then and Now," *Christian Register*, May 1932, p. 715.
9. Brown, "Brief History," p. 1.
10. "Harlem Pastor Defends Idealism," *New York Times*, August 11, 1948.
11. Brown, "Brief History," p. 1.
12. Egbert Ethelred Brown, *Amsterdam News*, n.p., n.d.
13. Lewis McGee, "Study of the South Side Negro Community of Chicago, IL (Commissioned by the American Unitarian Association, Spring 1948).
14. Gayraud S. Wilmore, *Black Religion and Black Radicalism* (Garden City, NY: Doubleday, 1972), p. 113.
15. "How 'Open' Is the Unitarian Door?" p. 12.
16. Howard Thurman, *With Head and Heart* (New York: Harcourt Brace Jovanovich, 1979), pp. 160-161.
17. The Reverend Edward H. Redman, interview in Washington, DC, in March 1983.

5: INTEGRATION WHERE IT COUNTS
1. Dan Dale and Eric Haugan, "Class and Conflict: The Declining Influence of Religion in Unitarian Universalism" (typescript, Spring 1978).
2. Robert Coles, "Work and Self-Respect," *Daedalus*, Fall 1976, pp. 29-38.
3. Stephen Steinberg, *The Ethnic Myth: Race, Ethnicity, and Class in America* (Boston: Beacon Press, 1981), p. 209.

6: "WHERE THERE IS NO VISION"
1. Douglas C. Stange, *Patterns of Antislavery Among American Unitarians, 1831-1860* (Cranbury, NJ: Asso-

ciated University Presses, Inc.) pp. 226-227.

2. Earl Morse Wilbur, *A History of Unitarianism: In Transylvania, England and America* (Boston: Beacon Press, 1952), p. 440.

3. Charles H. Lyttle, *Freedom Moves West: A History of Western Unitarian Conferences* (Boston: Beacon Press, 1952), p. 223.

4. Jeffrey Campbell, Interview in Putney, Vermont, July 1979.

5. Works Progress Administration, "Survey of State and Local Historical Records: 1936, Ohio Historical Records Survey," the Rev. William Carter interviewed by William Polasky, December 4, 1939.

6. *Cincinnati Enquirer*, W.H.G. Carter, Death Notice, May 29, 1962.

7. Memorandum to George G. Davis from Lon Ray Call, Subject: Unitarian Brotherhood Church, Negro, Cincinnati, Ohio, November 14, 1938.

8. Letter from Lon Ray Call to Mark Morrison-Reed, February 11, 1984.

9. Letter from Betty L. Reid to Hayward Henry, February 20, 1968.

7: HOW OPEN IS THE DOOR?
HOW LOUD IS THE CALL?

1. Commission on Appraisal, *The Quality of Religious Life in Unitarian Universalist Congregations* (Boston: UUA, 1989).

2. Donald Harrington, "John Haynes Holmes and the Cry for Social Justice and World Peace," sermon delivered at the Community Church of New York on March 16, 1965 (New York: Community Church, 1975), p. 15.

3. *Christian Register*, "Twelve Years' Persistence Achieves Integration After Chicago Church Overcomes Slow Start" (September, 1956), p. 26.

4. David M. Reimers, *White Protestantism and the Negro* (New York: Oxford University Press, 1965), p. 158.

5. Wallace P. Rusterholz, *The First Unitarian Society of*

Chicago: A Brief History (Chicago: First Unitarian Society, 1979), p. 15.

6. Conversation with James Luther Adams.
7. Report of the Commission on Unitarian Intergroup Relations, "How 'Open' Is the Unitarian Door?" *Christian Register* (April, 1954).
8. Interview of David H. Eaton by Carol Lynn Dornbrand, 1985.
9. David H. Eaton, "Racism Is Alive and Well," a Skinner Sermon delivered at All Souls Unitarian Church of Washington, DC, November 10, 1985 (Washington, DC: All Souls Unitarian Church).
10. Wade Clark Roof and William McKinney, *American Mainline Religion: Its Changing Shape and Future* (New Brunswick, London: Rutgers University Press, 1987), p. 64.
11. Roof and McKinney, p. 66.
12. Roof and McKinney, pp. 143-44.
13. David Maraniss, "Hard Choices in Black and White, A Church in Philadelphia Facing Racial Issues in a Liberal Religion," *The Washington Post* (March 5, 1990), p. A6.
14. Ibid.
15. Ibid.
16. Ibid.
17. Ibid.
18. Ibid.
19. Roof and McKinney, pp. 186-228.
20. Personal interview with Fern Gayten, Chicago, February 8, 1979.
21. Roof and McKinney, pp. 138, 144.
22. Eaton, "Racism Is Alive and Well," p. 6.
23. Pat DeBrady, *The Washington Post*.
24. Ethelred Brown, "Making Religion More Satisfying Emotionally," address delivered at a symposium of the Metropolitan Conference, May 16, 1954.

Selected Bibliography

American Unitarian Association. *Yearbooks*. Boston, 1908-1957.

Bellah, Robert. *The Broken Covenant*. New York: Seabury Press, 1975.

Bennett, Lerone, Jr. *Before the Mayflower*. Baltimore: Penguin Books, 1962.

____. "Howard Thurman: Twentieth-Century Holy Man." *Ebony*, February 1978, pp. 68-85.

Bennett, Robert A. "Black Episcopalians: A History from the Colonial Period to the Present." *Historical Magazine of the Protestant Episcopal Church*, vol. 43, no. 3 (September 1974): 231-245.

Brown, Egbert Ethelred. Papers. Unitarian Universalist Association Archives, Boston; Springarn Collection, Howard University, Washington, DC; Schomburg Center for Research in Black Culture, New York Public Library, New York City; Meadville/Lombard Theological School Archives, Chicago.

Carpenter, Victor Howard. "The Black Empowerment Controversy and the Unitarian Universalist Association: 1967-1970." Delivered as part of the Minn's Lectures at Arlington Street Church, Boston, March 1983.

Cassara, Ernest, ed. *Universalism in America*. Boston: Beacon Press, 1971.

Coles, Robert. "Work and Self-Respect." *Daedalus*, Fall 1976, pp. 29-38.

Cone, Cecil Wayne. *The Identity Crisis in Black Theology*. Nashville: African Methodist Episcopal Church, 1975.

Cone, James H. *God of the Oppressed*. New York: Seabury Press, 1975.

____. *The Spirituals and the Blues*. New York: Seabury Press, 1972.

Cornish, Francis E. F. *Louis Craig Cornish: Interpreter of Life*. Boston: Beacon Press, 1953.

Cronon, E. David. *Black Moses: The Story of Marcus Garvey and the U.N.I.A.* Second edition. Madison, WI: University of Wisconsin Press, 1968.

Cruse, Harold. *The Crisis of the Negro Intellectual*. New York: Morrow, 1967.

Davies, A. Powell. *Man's Vast Future: A Definition of Democracy*. New York: Farrar, Straus and Young, 1951.

Douglass, Frederick. *Life and Times of Frederick Douglass*. Revised edition 1892. Reprint. London: Crowell-Collier, 1962.

DuBois, W. E. B. *The Gift of Black Folk*. 1924. Reprint. New York: Washington Square Press, 1970.

——. *The Souls of Black Folk*. Greenwich, CT: Fawcett, 1961.

Erskine, Noel Leo. *Black People and the Reformed Church in America*. Reformed Church Press, 1978.

"Essays on Black Episcopalian and Black History in Nineteenth and Twentieth Century America." *Historical Magazine of the Protestant Episcopal Church*, vol. 49, no. 1 (March 1980): 3-83.

Franklin, John Hope. *From Slavery to Freedom*. New York: Knopf, 1967.

Gibson, Gordon O. "Unitarian Universalist and the Civil Rights Movement—What Did We Do, and What Can We Learn from What We Did?" Typescript, 1983.

Gilliam, Dorothy Butler. *Paul Robeson: All American*. Washington, DC: New Republic, 1976.

Hamilton, Charles V. *The Black Preacher in America*. New York: Morrow, 1972.

Higgins, Daniel. "The UUA and the Color Line." D.Min. diss. Meadville/Lombard Theological School, 1977.

Hill, Robert A., ed. *Marcus Garvey and United Negro Improvement Association Papers*. vol. 1. Berkeley: University of California Press, 1983.

Hoffer, Eric. *The True Believer*. New York: Harper & Row,

1951. Reprint. Perennial Library, 1966.

Holmes, John Haynes. Papers. Library of Congress, Washington, DC.

Jones, William R. *Is God a White Racist?* Garden City, NY: Anchor Press, 1973.

King, Martin Luther, Jr. *Strength to Love.* New York: Pocket Books, 1963.

Loescher, Frank S. *The Protestant Church and the Negro.* New York: Association Press, 1948.

Lyttle, Charles H. *Freedom Moves West.* Boston: Beacon Press, 1952.

May, Samuel J. *Recollections of the Antislavery Conflict.* Boston: Fields, Osgood & Co., 1869.

McClendon, James W. *Biography as Theology: How Life Stories Can Remake Today's Theology.* Nashville: Abingdon Press, 1974.

McCloskey, Michael. "Unitarian Universalism and Black Empowerment in the United States: A Nationwide Survey of Unitarian Universalist Attitudes toward Black Power and Participation in Militant Civil Rights Activities." Ph.D. diss. Loyola University of Chicago, 1974.

McGiffert, Arthur C., Jr. *Pilot of the Liberal Faith: Samuel Atkins Eliot, 1862-1950.* Boston: Beacon Press, 1976.

Mead, Sidney E. *The Lively Experiment.* New York: Harper & Row, 1963.

Miller, Perry. *Errand into the Wilderness.* Cambridge, MA: Harvard University Press, 1956.

Miller, Robert L'H. "The Religious Value System of Unitarian Universalist." *Review of Religious Research,* vol. 17, no. 3 (Spring 1976): 189-208.

Niebuhr, H. Richard. *The Social Sources of Denominationalism,* eleventh edition. New York: World Publishing Co., 1929.

Parke, David B. "Patterns of Power: Universalist and Unitarian Leadership Styles Since 1900." *The Right Time: The Best of Kairos,* edited by David B. Parke.

Boston: Skinner House, 1982.

___ . "A Wave at the Crest." in *A Stream of Light*, edited by Conrad Wright. Boston: Unitarian Universalist Association, 1975.

Record, Wilson. *The Negro and the Communist Party*. New York: Atheneum, 1971.

Redman, Edward H. Interview March 1983, Washington, DC.

Reimers, David M. *White Protestantism and the Negro*. New York: Oxford University Press, 1965.

Reist, Benjamin A. *Theology in Red, White, and Black*. Philadelphia: Westminster Press, 1975.

Rusterholtz, Wallace P. *The First Unitarian Society of Chicago: A Brief History*. Chicago: First Unitarian Church, 1979.

Samuels, Wilfred David. "Five Afro-Caribbean Voices in American Culture, 1917-1929: Hubert H. Harrison, Wilfred A. Domingo, Richard B. Moore, Cyril V. Briggs, and Claude McKay." PhD diss., University of Iowa, 1977.

Scott, Benjamin. *The Coming of the Black Man*. Boston: Beacon Press, 1968.

Steinberg, Stephen. *The Ethnic Myth: Race, Ethnicity, and Class in America*. Boston: Beacon Press, 1981.

Tapp, Robert. *Religion among the Unitarian Universalists*. New York: Seminar Press, 1973.

Thurman, Howard. *Footprints of a Dream*. New York: Harper & Brothers, 1959.

___ . *With Head and Heart*. New York: Harcourt Brace Jovanovich, 1979.

Unitarian Universalist Hymnbook Commission. *Hymns for the Celebration of Life*. Boston: Beacon Press, 1964.

Washington, Joseph R., Jr. *Black Religion*. Boston: Beacon Press, 1964.

Wilbur, Earl Morse. *A History of Unitarianism in Transylvania, England, and America*. Boston: Beacon Press, 1945.

Williams, George Huntston. *American Universalism*. Boston: Beacon Press, 1971.

Williams, Preston N. "Black Church: Origin, History, Present Dilemmas." *Andover-Newton Quarterly*, vol. 9, no. 2 (November 1968): 112-123.

Wilmore, Gayraud S. *Black Religion and Black Radicalism*. Garden City, NY: Doubleday, 1972.

World Tomorrow Magazine. Edited by Norman Thomas. Fellowship Press, 19? -1934.

INTERVIEWS

Campbell, The Reverend Jeffrey. Putney, VT. Interview, July 1979.

Cress, Ida. Chicago, IL. Interview, February 8, 1979.

Fleck, G. Peter. South Orleans, MA. Telephone interview, February 1979.

Gayten, Fern. Chicago, IL. Interview, February 8, 1979.

Goodloe, Wallis A. Bowie, MD. Telephone interview, November 19, 1982.

Gough, William. Chicago, IL. Interview, February 9, 1979.

Gudmundson, The Reverend Emil. Chicago, IL. Interview, February 6, 1979.

Harrington, The Reverend Donald S. New York, NY. Interview, January 8, 1978.

Henry, Beryl. Jamaica, NY. Interview, January 8, 1978.

Hilton, The Reverend Randall, and Gladys Hilton. Chicago, IL. Interview, February 7, 1979.

Jack, The Reverend Homer. New York, NY. Interview, December 4, 1978.

Jordan, Virginia. Flint, MI. Telephone interview, November 30, 1982.

Leslie, Dorice Brown. Jamaica, NY. Interview, December 4, 1978.

McGee, The Reverend Lewis, and Marcella McGee. Bethesda, MD. Interview, December 7, 1977. Pullman, WA. Telephone interviews, February 1979.

Morgan, The Reverend John. Toronto, Canada. Telephone interview, November 30, 1982.

Richardson, The Reverend Benjamin. Chicago, IL. Interview, November 29, 1978.
Tweedee, Wilson. Flint, MI. Telephone interviews, December 1982.

Index

251